Audit in the
Public Sector

Audit in the Public Sector

Second Edition

Roger Buttery   Managing Director,
Hartshead Limited and Vice President, CIPFA

Chris Hurford   Associate Director,
Audit Commission and Chairman, CIPFA Audit Panel

and

Robert K. Simpson   Former Controller of Audit,
Local Authority Accounts Commission for Scotland

Published in association with CIPFA

ICSA Publishing
The Official Publishing Company of
The Institute of Chartered Secretaries and Administrators

First published as *Internal Audit in the Public Sector* 1986
Then as *Audit in the Public Sector* 1989
This edition published 1993
ICSA Publishing Limited
Campus 400, Maylands Avenue
Hemel Hempstead
Hertfordshire, HP2 7EZ

Typeset in 10/12pt Times and Univers
by Hands Fotoset, Leicester

Printed and bound in Great Britain by
T.J. Press (Padstow) Ltd, Cornwall

British Library Cataloguing in Publication Data

A catalogue record for this book is available from
the British Library

ISBN 1-872860-60-5 (pbk)

1 2 3 4 5   97 96 95 94 93

Contents

Preface

The purpose of this book is to provide, under one cover, a concise but comprehensive guide to the principles and practical problems of both internal and external audit in the public sector. The book is aimed at both students and practitioners in all organisations providing public services including external auditors.

The public sector used to be clearly defined but in the past few years there has been a blurring of the public/private sector boundary. The public sector almost defies definition since its boundaries vary according to the criteria by which one wishes to describe it. It may or may not include, according to one's definition, the trading activities of 'public' bodies, some public corporations, the 'privatised' provision of public services and government grants to private industry.

The need for public services will remain, indeed grow. However, the arrangements for the delivery and management of these services has been changing and will continue to change. As a result:

- the role of the public sector as an enabler rather than provider will grow;
- responsibility for the delivery of more public services will be with the managers of private-style companies;
- commercial management styles and pressures will become increasingly important in the management processes;
- those services where delivery remains in the public sector may often be delivered by single-purpose institutions, sometimes quite small in size;
- the division between the purchaser and provider roles will increasingly dominate the delivery of those public services remaining within the public sector; and
- audit requirements will change with the increasing use of company style structures leading to a need for an audit qualification that is equally acceptable under Companies Act and public sector legislation.

Throughout the book, our aim has been to produce concise information on the full range of matters affecting internal audit in the public services, covering such issues as its role and objectives, auditing standards, audit management, competition in the provision of internal audit services, audit documentation, conduct of an audit, fraud and corruption, value for money, specialist areas such as contract and computer audit and national developments. In view of the nature of this publication, references to audit techniques and particular types of audit have been kept to a minimum, although the principal techniques are identified and examples are provided of internal control questionnaires and audit programmes.

As before, this edition of the book includes a section (Part II) on external audit. Much of what is said in the context of internal audit applies equally to external auditors, the differences between the two disciplines relating more to emphasis than to objectives. There is a chapter giving a general introduction to external audit supported by chapters on the Audit Commission, Scottish Accounts Commission, Northern Ireland, the National Audit Office, the regulated utilities, Education and finally Housing.

From time to time, the book draws on the work undertaken by the Chartered Institute of Public Finance and Accountancy, and we are grateful to the Institute for allowing us this facility.

August 1993

Roger Buttery
Chris Hurford
Robert K. Simpson

Acknowledgements

We acknowledge and are very grateful to the following for their assistance in the production of parts of the book and, in certain instances, for allowing us to reproduce material:

Chartered Institute of Public Finance and Accountancy
Auditing Practices Board
Mike Barnes, The Audit Commission
John Broadfoot, Controller, Accounts Commission for Scotland
Jack Bailie, Chief Local Government Auditor for Northern Ireland
Phil Woodhead, National Audit Office
Ken Odgers, Corporation of London

PART I

Internal Audit

CHAPTER 1

The role and objectives of internal audit

Introduction

Internal audit is an integral part of the financial structure of organisations providing public services. Most public authorities recognised the importance of internal audit many years ago, some of the larger ones adopting it in the early years of this century, and today very few, if any, organisations providing public services operate without some form of internal audit. Over the years, however, the precise role of internal audit has changed. In the early days, its primary responsibility was concerned with the detection and prevention of errors and fraud, with perhaps an overdue concentration on examining accounts before payment, collecting income and checking petty cash claims. Today, (internal audit operates in a more dynamic environment with an emphasis on reviewing systems of internal control. Internal audit exists within organisations to carry out an independent appraisal of the effectiveness of internal controls, financial and other, operating within each organisation.)

Over the years, various organisations have produced statements on, and definitions of, the role and objectives of internal audit. For the purpose of this book, the *Guidance for Internal Auditors*, published in 1990 by the former Auditing Practices Committee (APC) of the Consultative Committee of Accounting Bodies (CCAB), has been used.

As the Auditing Practices Board (APB) has taken over responsibility for all APC publications, the APC's *Guidance for Internal Auditors* is referred to throughout this book as the APB guideline. The role of the APB is explained more fully in Chapter 2.

The APB's guideline replaces the 'role and objectives' statement published in 1979 by the Chartered Institute of Public Finance and Accountancy (CIPFA). CIPFA is one of the six major professional accountancy bodies in the United Kingdom and is the premier body which specialises in financial management for organisations providing public services.

Internal audit and internal control

The Auditing Practices Board (APB) guideline defines internal audit as an independent appraisal function established by the management of an organisation for the review of the internal control system as a service to the organisation. It objectively examines, evaluates and reports on the adequacy of internal control as a contribution to the proper, economic, efficient and effective use of resources. Regrettably, the 'independent appraisal function' has not been accepted by all public sector organisations. For example, some organisations do not have separate internal audit sections engaged solely on audit duties. In this situation, internal audit is part of the departmental systems and procedures, which means a consequential loss in audit's effectiveness. As a further example, some internal audit sections are responsible for monitoring the regularity of banking, administering car loans or checking every pension benefit. This is a complete misuse of internal audit's resources.

One of the reasons for this state of affairs is that there is confusion over internal audit and internal control. Internal control is the whole set of controls initiated by management designed to enable the organisation to perform its objectives in a safe, secure, and accurate as well as efficient manner. Internal control is quite clearly management's responsibility.

Internal audit is not a substitute for good management and it is in this area that misunderstandings have arisen. Consequently, the manager of an organisation providing public service is responsible for the whole system of financial and other controls which are established within his department to safeguard its assets, ensure reliability of records, promote operational efficiency and monitor adherence to policies and objectives. Audit's role is to provide management with an independent view on the system and procedures and assess whether the standards are achieved in a secure and efficient manner.

In the past, and even today in some organisations, internal audit still works to narrow terms of reference and continues to concentrate on appraising, for example, the accuracy of income and petty cash and the propriety of creditors. Whilst this aspect will always be an important feature of the control function, it must not be allowed to dominate internal audit's activities. Internal audit's responsibilities are much wider and, as an absolute minimum, it is essential that the principal internal control systems are properly appraised and that a report on their effectiveness is made to management.

Independence

For an organisation providing public services to achieve the maximum benefit from the activities of internal audit, it is essential that the auditor should not be engaged in any system which would normally be reviewed and appraised.

Internal audit activity should not be restricted and auditors should have full rights of access to records, assets and personnel, and receive such information and explanations as they consider necessary for the performance of their duties. (The whole question of independence is discussed in Chapter 3.)

Client's view of internal audit

Audit is now operating in a more competitive environment and more attention is being directed towards the role of audit services. One of the primary objectives of the Audit Panel of CIPFA is to promote and enhance the discipline and image of audit. A vital step in planning how best to achieve this target is to understand the perceptions of the customer of audit services. With this in mind, the Audit Panel commissioned a survey amongst managers from a broad cross-section of organisations in both the public and private sectors, and incorporated the views of chief officers or managing directors, treasurers or finance directors and service departments' managers.

The objective of the survey was to identify managers' perceptions of their internal audit service, at present and as they see it developing in the future. From this, the Audit Panel sought to identify the key issues which internal audit must address in order to meet the challenges of the future. The following is an executive summary of the Research Report largely reproduced from *The Client's View of Internal Audit*.

Analysis of the survey results identified a number of positive messages from which internal audit can draw encouragement. It has also, however, identified a number of consistent themes which represent the key issues facing internal audit. The themes identified are:

- the value of internal audit;
- status;
- independence;
- role;
- quality;
- organisational relationships;
- training; and
- image.

Many of these themes are interrelated, and should not therefore be viewed as issues in isolation. However, after analysing the results of the survey within the context of these themes, priorities can be identified for internal audit in terms of the action required to respond to the views expressed by their clients, and recommendations have been proposed which should provide the way forward for internal audit.

The most important message arising from the survey is that the majority of client managers value their internal audit service and consider it to be essential to their organisation. This is supported by the fact that managers generally feel that internal audit makes a positive contribution to the management of their departments; that it understands the real issues confronting their organisations; and that it is capable of discussing and assisting with technical issues.

Managers also perceive a growing need for internal audit in the future, particularly in view of the increasing use of computerised systems. This encouraging response is further supported by the fact that most managers are happy with their relationship with internal audit. Furthermore, there are positive comments regarding the present quality of the internal audit service, both in the aspect of reports, and in a wider context, such as the professionalism of internal audit staff.

Despite the positive messages, two important challenges facing internal audit have emerged. There is a strong need for internal audit to promote its services to its 'clients' more effectively, but, perhaps equally importantly, internal audit must first develop the services it is promoting. A number of issues such as the status and image of internal audit, the quality of its service, its relationships with clients and its perceived value to management will be effectively addressed only if client managers are better persuaded of the role of internal audit and the benefits and skills which it has to offer.

There is a view, held by many managers, that internal audit must offer a wider range of services in the future. Although there is a clear need to retain the probity and regularity role of audit, there is also an increasing demand for other services, such as value for money work, computer audit and system review. Meeting this challenge will be vital for internal audit, and will require attention to be focused on a number of the other key issues raised by this survey.

Amongst the most important of these is the need to provide relevant ongoing training and career development programmes for internal auditors at all levels. The provision of services such as value for money and computer audit requires a broader range of auditing and technical skills than those traditionally displayed by auditors in the past.

Senior management within the organisation needs to be better aware of the role of internal audit and it is opportune that the CCAB's Auditing Practices Board has published its *Guidance for Internal Auditors* which sets down, for all internal auditors in the public and private sectors, guidance on the role and responsibilities of internal audit. If client management understands the opportunities which an effective internal audit department can offer its organisation, then it is more likely to give that audit department the support and facilities which it will need to deliver the service expected of it.

The quality of internal audit's relationships with its clients is crucial to its effective operation. Generally, chief officers and financial managers expressed satisfaction with, for example, the degree of influence which they are able to exert over the level and quality of internal audit services. This view was not shared, however, by non-financial managers. This issue must be of concern to internal audit, particularly if, as is suggested, they will be expected to provide a wider range of services in the future, and therefore extend their involvement into new areas of the organisation.

Internal audit's relationships with other review agencies, such as management services, are also regarded as requiring improvement. Again, this is not an easy problem to address, but the perceived value to management of internal audit can be enhanced only if this type of relationship is seen to be operating well.

There is much to be done. The analysis of the survey results shows that the current state of internal audit varies between organisations, some of which are in a better position than others. There are few, if any, that can afford to be complacent, and the survey results provide an excellent opportunity to lead internal audit forward.

CHAPTER 2
Auditing standards

Background

For many years, accountancy and auditing bodies have striven to enhance the performance and quality of both internal and external audit by the introduction of auditing standards. This is a term employed to denote authoritative guidance which prescribes the basic principles and practices that auditors should follow during the conduct of an audit.

Some of the bodies introduced their own statements or standards of audit. For example, in 1979 CIPFA published *Statements on Internal Audit Practice – Public Sector*. Shortly afterwards, the Institute of Internal Auditors issued *Standards for the Professional Practice of Internal Auditing*, which was closely followed by *Standards for Government Internal Audit*, published by HM Treasury.

The Auditing Practices Committee (APC) was established in 1976 as a Committee of the Consultative Committee of Accountancy Bodies (CCAB) to advance standards of auditing in the profession. It chose to effect this by issuing guidance on the best auditing practice on a number of levels which, in order of status, were as follows:

1. Auditing standards.
2. Auditing guidelines.
3. Audit briefs.
4. True and fair bulletins.

The first of the APC's auditing standards and guidelines, published in April 1980, was mainly a codification of existing best practice. Although addressed primarily to professional auditors in the private sector, the guidance contained much of equal relevance in the public sector.

Throughout the APC's existence, over thirty auditing standards and guidelines were issued on a wide variety of audit topics. Some dealt with general principles (e.g. planning, controlling and recording) and are capable of being applied to all audits. Others applied only in certain circumstances (e.g. attendance at stocktakings) or are addressed to particular industries (e.g. charities or housing associations).

In the mid 1980s, the APC created its public sector initiative to ensure that public sector considerations were taken into account as appropriate in the preparation of all APC guidance. In addition, the APC considered the feasibility of producing guidance on topics of particular relevance to the public sector but which were also applicable to the wider profession. This culminated with the issue in 1990 of the auditing guideline, *Guidance for Internal Auditors*. It applies to internal auditors in both the public and private sectors and replaces CIPFA's *Statements on Internal Practice – Public Sector*.

The principles enunciated in the guideline are intended to apply to all internal audits conducted by all public and private sector organisations, irrespective of their size. The guidelines prescribe basic principles and practices which should be followed in the conduct of all internal audits where the auditor is called upon to express an opinion upon the soundness, adequacy and application of internal control, and to report independently thereon. The guidelines include:

- objectives and scope of internal audit;
- independence;
- staffing and training;
- relationships;
- due care;
- planning, controlling and recording;
- evaluation of the internal control system;
- evidence; and
- reporting and follow-up.

As can be seen from these headings, the subjects covered by the guidelines are dealt with in some depth in various chapters of this book. It is not necessary, therefore, to deal with each guideline in any detail in this chapter; however, all the guidelines are reproduced for information in Appendix 1.

It must be recognised that standards in themselves achieve very little. They are, at most, a catalogue of best practice. Standards must be implemented after they have been produced. To be effective, they must be adopted by audit management and widely publicised and distributed amongst staff; most important of all, compliance with them must be closely monitored as an integral part of quality control.

Developments

The Auditing Practices Board (APB) was established by the CCAB in April

1991 as the successor body to the APC. The establishment of the APB followed a thorough review of the arrangements for setting auditing standards and guidelines, in response to criticisms that the APC was too dominated by the accountancy profession and the major accountancy firms.

The two key features of the new board are: firstly, it is independent of the CCAB; and, secondly, its membership has been widened to include non-auditors.

Members of the APB are appointed by a selection committee, comprising the Presidents of the CCAB members, and nominees put forward by the Governor of the Bank of England and by the Stock Exchange. In the past, each CCAB body was allowed to nominate a certain number of representatives without further scrutiny. The APB has authority to issue auditing standards and guidelines after due consultation, without seeking the approval of the CCAB bodies. Therefore, the CCAB bodies no longer have a veto on the issue of standards and guidelines as they had in the past.

The Board comprises eighteen voting members, of whom one half are practitioners and the other half non-practitioners. The non-practitioners include 'persons of standing' in the business world, academy and the law. The membership includes nominees from the Bank of England, the Stock Exchange and the Securities and Investments Board (SIB). The public sector is represented by nominees from the National Audit Office and the Audit Commission.

APB statement of objectives

The APB is committed to leading the development of auditing practice in the United Kingdom and the Republic of Ireland so as to:

- establish the highest standards of auditing;
- meet the developing needs of users of financial information; and
- ensure public confidence in the auditing process.

To achieve these objectives, the APB intends to:

- take an active role in the development of statutes, regulations and accounting standards which affect the audit profession;
- promote ways of increasing the value of audits and of ensuring their cost-effectiveness;
- consult with the users of financial information to ensure that the APB provides an effective and timely response to their developing needs and to issues raised by them;
- advance the wider public's understanding of the roles and responsibilities of auditors; and

● establish and publish statements of the principles and procedures with which auditors are required to comply in the conduct of audits, and other explanatory material to assist in their interpretation and application. Pronouncements will have due regard to international developments.

The scope and authority of APB pronouncements

The pronouncements of the APB fall into two principal categories:

1. Statements of auditing standards (SASs).
2. Practice notes.

The scope and authority of the two types of pronouncement and the distinction between them are explained below. The APB also issues consultative documents and research studies to stimulate public debate and comment on matters of auditing practice.

Scope of statements of auditing standards (SASs)

SASs contain basic principles and essential procedures (auditing standards), with which auditors are required to comply in the conduct of any audit. SASs also include explanatory and other material which is designed to assist auditors in interpreting and applying auditing standards.

In addition to SASs of general application the APB issues SASs containing additional principles and procedures with which auditors are required to comply in the conduct of certain types of audit, such as the audits of entities within specialised industries. Each SAS specifies the date from which it becomes effective.

Authority of auditing standards

The members of CCAB have undertaken to adopt all SASs promulgated by the APB. Apparent failures by auditors to comply with SASs are liable for investigations by the appropriate committee established under the authority of the relevant accountancy body, and disciplinary or regulatory action may result.

In order to be eligible for appointment as auditors in Great Britain under the Companies Act 1985, persons must be registered with a supervisory body recognised under the Companies Act 1989 (a recognised supervisory body or RSB) and must be eligible for appointment under the rules of that RSB. The Companies Act 1989 requires RSBs to have rules and practices as to the technical standards to be applied in company audit work and as to the manner in which these standards are to be applied in practice.

Each RSB adopts SASs in order to meet that requirement and each is required to have arrangements in place for the effective monitoring and enforcement of compliance with those standards.

Auditors who do not comply with auditing standards when performing Companies Act audits make themselves liable to regulatory action which may include the withdrawal of registration. Furthermore it is understood that failure to apply relevant SASs in audits not carried out under companies legislation is a factor which an RSB will take into account when deciding whether persons are fit and proper to be eligible under its rules for appointment as company auditors.

In the Republic of Ireland legislative requirements concerning qualification for appointment as auditor and recognition of bodies of accountants are contained in the Companies Act 1990. The relevant sections are to be brought into force by ministerial order. In any event, members of the accountancy bodies in the Republic of Ireland are subject to the monitoring, enquiry and disciplinary procedures established under the authority of these bodies.

Auditing standards are likely to be taken into account when the adequacy of the work of auditors is being considered in a court of law or in other contested situations.

Departure from auditing standards

SASs cannot cater for all situations and circumstances which auditors might encounter. However, if auditors consider it necessary in exceptional circumstances to depart from auditing standards, they should disclose the matter in their report and be aware that any such decision may be subjected to enquiry or challenge.

Development of SASs

The APB is committed to wide consultation in the preparation of SASs. Prior to issuing SASs, the APB issues exposure drafts for general public comment and may issue other consultative documents in relation to proposed SASs. The APB also seeks out those with a special expertise or interest in the topic under consideration for consultation where necessary. The approval of at least three-quarters of the voting members of the APB is required before a SAS can be issued.

International standards on auditing (ISAs)

The APB supports the International Auditing Practices Committee of the

International Federation of Accountants (IFAC) in its aim of improving the degree of harmonisation of auditing practices throughout the world. SASs are formulated with due regard to international developments, in particular incorporating the principles on which are based the International Standards on Auditing (ISAs) issued by IFAC. Each SAS explains how it relates to the ISA dealing with the same topic. In most cases, complying with an SAS ensures compliance with the relevant ISA. Where the requirements of an SAS and an ISA differ, the SAS should be complied with in respect of audits of entities reporting within the United Kingdom and the Republic of Ireland.

Practice notes

The APB also issues practice notes to provide auditors with timely guidance on new or emerging issues, *and* to provide explanatory and other material to assist auditors in the interpretation and application of auditing standards.

Practice notes of both categories are indicative of good practice, even though they may be developed without the full process of consultation and exposure used for SASs. Hence practice notes are persuasive rather than prescriptive and have a lower level of authority than SASs.

Future developments

Against a background of growing concern and public scepticism about the value of the audit function, particularly in the wake of large-scale financial scandals, a number of initiatives are being pursued by the APB and other bodies. In 1992 the APB published a consultative paper, 'The future development of auditing – a paper to promote public debate', which suggested some ways of making company auditors' reports more informative and also for enlarging the groups whose interests should be recognised by auditors. It also emphasised that the current litigious environment militates against a wider role and scope for audit. The discussion on these and related issues will continue for some time; while the focus is upon company auditors, there are implications for external auditors performing under other legislation and for internal auditors too.

The Committee on the Financial Aspects of Corporate Governance chaired by Sir Adrian Cadbury (the Cadbury Committee) recommended that auditors of a listed company should have the following new responsibilities:

1. To review a statement by the directors of whether the company complies with the code of best practice set out in the Cadbury Report.
2. To report on a statement by the directors on the effectiveness of the internal control systems.

3. To report on a statement by the directors that the business is a going concern.
4. To review the company's interim report and discuss their findings with the audit committee.

European Commission's eighth directive

Part II of the Companies Act 1989 gives effect to the eighth directive on the regulation of auditors. It establishes a regime for the recognition by the Secretary of State for Industry of qualifying and supervisory bodies for auditors of company accounts. Among the principal features of the regime are provisions requiring a recognised supervisory body to have rules relating to the control of audit firms, professional integrity and independence, the application of technical standards, and the maintenance of competence in the conduct of audit work. A recognised supervisory body is also required to have arrangements for the effective monitoring and enforcement of its rules. Auditors must also take reasonable steps to secure that they are able to meet claims against them arising out of company audit work. The Act provides that this may be achieved by professional indemnity insurance or other appropriate arrangements. Provision is also made for the keeping of a register of auditors.

Readers will appreciate that the national situation is subject to changing developments. It follows that the authors can only reflect the position at the time of writing. The book will be subject to review, but some of the developments occur fairly rapidly and it may be necessary to ascertain the precise situation from time to time from journals such as *Public Finance and Accountancy*.

The authors acknowledge and are very grateful to the Auditing Practices Board for permission to reproduce most of the material for this chapter.

CHAPTER 3
The organisation of internal audit

Independence of audit

The APB guideline regards independence as one of the essentials for effective internal auditing and says that 'the internal auditor should have the independence in terms of organisational status and personal objectivity which permits the proper performance of his duties'. Paragraph 13 of the guideline emphasises this further by stating that 'each internal auditor should have an objective attitude of mind and be in a sufficiently independent position to be able to exercise judgement, express opinions and present recommendations with impartiality'.

Independence embraces such issues as:

- scope;
- access;
- report;
- activity;
- personnel; and
- attitude.

Let us examine these in turn.

Independence of scope

The scope of the auditor's work should not be restricted in any way. The auditor should be free to examine and report upon the activities of any department and any part of any department within the organisation. Obviously, attention should be drawn to delicate issues and sensitive areas, and regard must be had to these in formulating work programmes; nevertheless, the decision to include or exclude an area of activity should rest with the audit manager and should not be taken by anyone with a direct or indirect vested interest.

Independence of access

In order to carry out audit tasks fully, the auditor must have an unchallengeable right of access at all reasonable times to all financial and associated records of the organisation. There must be a right to examine all assets, including land and buildings, stocks and stores, investment certificates, transport and plant, furniture and fittings and cash. The auditor must be able to require any explanations that are deemed necessary from any employees.

Independence of report

The audit manager should be able to report, both verbally and in writing, to all levels of the organisation. Equally important, for those not attached to the department, is a direct line of communication to the chief executive which will greatly enhance the impact, and thus the effectiveness, of the audit function.

Independence of activity

Auditors should never become involved in the operation of any system upon which they will ultimately be required to report. Since auditors should be able to report upon any aspect of financial or management control, it follows that they should never become involved in any such activities. Nevertheless, it is quite common to find audit sections involved in controlling financial stationery (cheques, receipts, tickets, etc.), clearing receipting machines, processing invoices for payment, designing financial systems and in many other ways becoming directly involved in systems which they should be responsible for reviewing. Quite often such involvement is because of an emergency, such as staff shortages and peaks of work. Some directors of finance still see audit as an 'available pool of labour' which can readily be called upon to assist in such emergencies, however much that might compromise audit's independence. In the recent past, it became fashionable to combine audit with other activities, such as accounting, to form joint sections. Fortunately, this practice has virtually died out because of the conflict of interests which it created and also, predictably, because audit work took second place to the activity with which it was linked, since that activity inevitably had externally imposed deadlines. Resource difficulties should not result in this practice being resurrected.

Independence of personnel

This aspect of the concept of audit independence is less easy to arrange in practice, and the smaller the organisation, the more difficult it becomes. Often the audit manager will have to make the best arrangements possible within the constraints. The ideal to achieve is that the audit staff are totally independent of the staff who operate the systems under review. Audit staff should not be required to examine and report upon work done by persons with whom they are related or with whom they have a personal relationship. Similarly, audit staff should not be asked to audit an area of activity in which they themselves have had line management responsibility in the past.

Independence of attitude

An independent attitude is perhaps the single factor which can exert the greatest of impact upon the independence of the audit function. Perhaps it can be best described as a quality which incorporates 'single-mindedness', tempered by a cautious awareness of the views of others.

The audit manager

The post of audit manager (or chief internal auditor) is an important one in any organisation providing public services. It must be of a sufficient status to command respect throughout the organisation. In a book of this nature, it is not possible to be specific about this status. For one reason, the precise location of internal audit may vary between organisations. In many organisations, internal audit is usually located in the finance department and the audit manager is responsible to the head of finance who has a responsibility for the provision of internal audit. In other organisations providing public services, however, internal audit may be part of the chief executive's, managing director's or general manager's department. Another arrangement is for the audit manager to report to the board member for finance or direct to an Audit Committee.

The post of audit manager carries a great deal of managerial responsibility and requires making many decisions without the need to refer operational problems to a higher authority. It also involves contact and discussion, sometimes critical, with high-ranking officers of other departments and, on occasion, with board members. It is essential that the duties and responsibilities of the post are clearly defined. A typical job description of an audit manager or chief internal auditor is set out as follows:

JOB DESCRIPTION

Chief internal auditor in the public sector

1. Management responsibilities

   The chief internal auditor will be responsible for managing a highly qualified internal audit section comprising the following:

   (a) Qualified staff.

(b) Part-qualified staff.

(c) Unqualified staff and trainees.

He or she will be responsible for their recruitment and for organising a proper training programme involving a co-ordinated use of external courses and 'in-house' training.

2. Objectives

The objectives of internal audit are contained in financial regulations and are consistent with the APB's 'role and objectives of internal audit' statement and are embodied in the auditing guideline, *Guidance for Internal Auditors*. The chief internal auditor will be responsible for ensuring that these objectives are achieved.

3. Planning and supervision

The chief internal auditor will be required, at intervals not to exceed three years, to prepare a long-term audit plan, reconciling the staff resources available with the audit tasks to be completed and identifying the main areas of risk. The long-term plan will be submitted to (see footnote 1) for approval and will be kept constantly under review.

The chief internal auditor will also complete an annual detailed plan which he or she will be required to co-ordinate with that of the external auditor. This plan also will be submitted to (see footnote 1) for approval.

The chief internal auditor will arrange for the proper supervision and review of audit work and will ensure that the agreed audit plan is adhered to.

4. Reporting

The chief internal auditor will be responsible to (see footnote 2) but will have the facility to report under his or her own name on any matter connected with the organisation to any person within the organisation. Copies of all reports have to be submitted to (see footnote 2).

The chief internal auditor will prepare an annual report on the progress and activities of the internal audit section and this will have to be submitted to (see footnote 3) by a specified date.

5. Relationships

The chief internal auditor will be responsible for ensuring that good working relationships are established and maintained with all executive and central support departments. In particular, the chief internal auditor will ensure that a positive response is forthcoming in respect of matters raised by his or her section.

The chief internal auditor will also ensure that proper lines of communication are maintained with other review agencies such as external audit and management services, in order to avoid duplication and to maximise the use of resources.

The chief internal auditor will maintain close links with the police and will be responsible for referring all frauds and irregularities, after consultation with appropriate officers.

6. Professional responsibility

The chief internal auditor will be required to keep up to date on legislation changes and developments within the auditing profession. He or she will ensure that his or her staff are apprised of all relevant changes.

Footnote 1 The person to whom the audit plans are submitted will depend upon the specific management structure. It may be to the director of finance, to the chief executive or to a board member.

Footnote 2 Ideally, the chief internal auditor should be responsible to the director of finance, to the chief executive or to a board member and copies of all reports should be submitted to that person.

Footnote 3 The annual report will normally be submitted to the person to whom the chief internal auditor is responsible. However, it would also be advantageous to supply copies to the finance committee or to the board.

Size of audit section

Very little guidance is available to the audit manager to assist in determining how large the audit section should be. This is really not surprising since there are so many variables as to make such guidance impossible to produce, except in the broadest of terms. The following is a list of just some of the variables which must be taken into account in fixing the size of a section.

- *The role of the audit section* How wide a role does management envisage for its internal audit function?
- *The quality and experience of the staff* The more experienced the staff, generally, the fewer that are needed to carry out the task.
- *The geography of the area* Auditors covering a wide geographical area will spend much more time travelling and, consequently, more manpower resources will be needed to achieve the same level of coverage.
- *The standard of systems of financial control* Far fewer auditors are needed to look after a 'tight ship'.
- *The rate of development* A dynamic organisation will require more audit input into reviewing developing systems.
- *The degree of automation/computerisation* This can have a profound effect upon the level of input and, indeed, upon its nature.
- *The extent to which fringe activities are carried out* These can be handled by other review agencies (e.g. management services).
- *The extent to which activities are centralised* It is often easier to review a centralised function than to examine the same function carried out in a large number of outstations.

Rarely is the audit manager faced with a 'blank sheet of paper', except where a new organisation has been formed or where an audit section is to be developed where one previously did not exist. In such cases, some guidance can be obtained by referring to similar-sized organisations, with the same functions, where as many as possible of the variables fall within the same range. However, in the majority of cases an audit manager will seek to compare the size of the section with others when he considers that there are insufficient resources to meet the workplan. By far the most effective means of doing this is through a detailed audit plan which expresses clearly the risks which management are incurring by restricting the size of the audit section.

Audit staffing and structure

The staffing and structure of an audit section will, like its size, depend to a large extent on local factors. Indeed, the size of the section will itself help to determine the type of staffing and structure, as will many of the factors which influenced the size of the section. In addition to these, however, the extent to which computer systems are used, the structure and staffing of the organisation and, in particular, the finance department, and the concentration on specific aspects, such as capital expenditure or value for money, are factors to be borne in mind when organising the audit section.

Ideally, within an audit section, there should be a blend of experience, up-to-date knowledge, initiative, drive and tact. Most audit section staff are predominantly accountants, whether qualified, part-qualified or trainees. Some sections, however, favour the multi-disciplined approach, so in addition to accountants they employ, for example, engineers and operational research specialists. The career structure for finance staff is not generally based on the internal audit section but on the finance department as a whole. This leads to staff being transferred in and out of the audit section, which can cause problems on occasions, particularly if experienced staff leave. It is important, therefore, that there is sufficient incentive, in the form of adequate remuneration and job satisfaction, for experienced staff to remain in the section.

In addition to staff engaged in traditional audit duties, there is a growing need for auditors to specialise in particular activities. Perhaps the best example of this is computer audit, although, in the larger organisations, the time is rapidly approaching when all auditors should have experience in this aspect. Other specialist areas might include contract audit and energy management.

The staff of the audit section will normally be organised into audit teams, each headed by a team or group leader. The division of staff may be based on services (e.g. education in a local authority) or on functions (payroll, income, etc.) or a combination of both. Each team should be responsible for the completion of part of the audit plan and the group leaders will be involved in the compilation of this plan. Group leaders should also have some responsibility for the administration of the internal audit section as a whole, as well as for their own particular team, and should be involved in the determination of overall audit policy.

Recruitment and training

The training of audit staff is a costly business and one which, unfortunately, does not receive sufficient attention in many organisations. In this section the personal qualities, for which the audit manager should be looking when recruiting audit staff, will be examined briefly before training is discussed further.

Personal qualities

Auditors of long standing will be tempted to say that the only personal quality required of an auditor is perfection. It is true, however, that a higher degree of personal qualities is required of an auditor than of staff in many other disciplines. The following are the most important personal qualities:

- *Intelligence* If an auditor is to acquire the wide-ranging skills and techniques necessary then the individual must undoubtedly possess a sound intellect which needs to be balanced with a high degree of common sense.
- *Tenacity* While this is an important quality needed by an auditor it does need to be tempered with judgement. Too many auditors hold on tenaciously to an exhausted line of investigation.
- *An inquiring mind* An inquisitive nature, combined with a tendency not to accept information at face value without challenge, are vital qualities for an auditor.
- *Imagination* Auditors need to have an imaginative approach to their work, particularly those involved with reviews of economy, efficiency and effectiveness (i.e. value for money). Audit managers should select staff who can demonstrate a creative and innovative attitude.
- *Good behavioural qualities* An auditor should have the ability to get on well with colleagues and those with whom he/she comes into contact through audit work. Few professions test the behavioural qualities of an individual more than auditing, and much emphasis needs to be placed on this aspect when recruiting audit staff.
- *Commitment* The very nature of auditing work dictates that practitioners need to be largely self-motivated. Thus, whilst it is not always possible to recruit staff who regard auditing as a vocation, there should always be a discernible commitment to the objectives of audit.
- *Communication* The successful auditor will need good verbal and written communication skills.

- *Good character* It goes without saying that an auditor should have an impeccable character.

Training

It is true to say that in many professions training does not have as high a priority as it deserves and audit is no exception. At a time of severely limited resources, training is often regarded as an expendable luxury. On the other hand, it is fair to say that the last twenty years have seen a dramatic improvement in audit skills and techniques in the public services and much of this can be attributed to the training efforts of CIPFA, both nationally and through its regional structure. The deficiencies have tended to lie in the field of 'in-service' training.

Objectives of training

Before the practicalities of developing a training programme are explored, it is first necessary to examine the objectives of training audit staff. Broadly speaking, the training programme should have as its aim the development of a wide range of audit skills, as follows:

- *Basic technical skills* These include flowcharting, analytical skills, use of audit programmes and internal control questionnaires, production of satisfactory working papers, and audit report writing.
- *Professional skills* These include a knowledge of accountancy and relevant legislation.
- *Specialist technical skills* These include computer audit techniques and contract audit skills.
- *Investigatory skills* These include how to conduct a value-for-money study and how to investigate fraud and corruption.
- *Human behavioural skills* These include interviewing techniques, how to deal with an awkward auditee and how to persuade management to accept audit recommendations.
- *Management and organisational skills* These include how to conduct an audit, how to lead an audit team, and audit planning and control.
- *Knowledge of an organisation* This includes knowing the protocol, regulations, procedures and the decision-making processes of an organisation and knowing how it is structured.

The training programme

The development of a programme which will impart the various skills outlined above is no easy task and clearly not all members of staff will require the whole range of skills. A useful starting point, therefore, is to identify the skill requirements of each member of the section and thereby to assess the training needs. There are distinct advantages in involving staff in the process of identification; often their perception of their own training needs differs from that of the audit manager and may even be more accurate.

Training can conveniently be divided into four broad categories, as follows:

1. Practical experience.
2. Professional training.
3. In-service training.
4. External training.

The training programme should encompass each of these.

Practical experience

Often, too little regard is given to the importance of practical experience as an integral part of a training programme. The old expression that much can be learned 'sitting next to Nellie' contains a great deal of truth. Obviously, getting through the work programme is of paramount importance but, as far as is possible without interfering too much in the flow of work, staff should be given as wide an experience as possible at all levels. A surprising number of training objectives can be met in this way.

Professional training

Obviously, this will be restricted to those members of staff who are studying for the professional examinations of one of the major accountancy bodies. (In the public sector, the body will normally be CIPFA.) Auditing forms only a part of the syllabus and therefore such a course is designed to develop a broad appreciation of the skills and techniques needed by the professional auditor. The audit manager can expect that such a course will cover the 'basic technical skills' and 'professional skills' mentioned earlier and will provide a foundation to the other areas of need.

In-service training

The in-service training programme should aim to provide a working knowledge of the organisation and to develop those other skills for which external training is not available. In-service programmes will vary considerably, therefore, and it is only possible to provide very broad guidance as to the sorts of areas which might be covered. A growing trend is for 'shared' programmes, where two or more organisations join together to run such a programme. This is particularly useful where a number of adjacent small organisations find that, individually, they do not possess the necessary resources to provide in-service training.

An essential part of any in-service training programme is an induction course for new entrants which is aimed at providing the basic audit skills and a broad appreciation of the organisation. Delegates should emerge knowing the objectives of audit, their own part in the process and, hopefully, what to do if they identify a serious problem.

Many audit managers find it useful to designate a specific day each month for in-service training in order that audit work can be planned accordingly; and, whilst it is not always possible to include topics which will be useful to all levels of audit staff, it is of great benefit, on occasion, to hold combined sessions which involve all levels in the organisation. Apart from creating a good team spirit, the junior members of the team will gain much from the experienced participation of the senior audit staff.

Another possible avenue of in-service training, which is particularly useful for large audit organisations with geographically based teams which rarely meet, is an annual conference. In this way staff can come together in a relaxed atmosphere to share problems and ideas and to participate in a programme of concentrated training.

The following are typical topics relating to an organisation which are covered by in-service training sessions:

- Standing orders and financial regulations.
- Accounting and budgetary control.
- The decision-making process.
- The organisation and management of audit.
- Preparation for an audit.
- Conduct of an audit.
- Protocol and reporting lines.

The following are some more general topics covered:

- Systems audit.
- Audit testing and techniques.
- Internal control questionnaires.
- Flowcharting.
- Report writing and audit documentation.
- Industrial relations and the auditor.
- Interviewing and the judges' rules.

External training

Many forms of external training are available and the audit manager is often bombarded with leaflets advertising courses run by professional bodies, academic institutions and, increasingly, by speculative private organisations. The public sector is also well served by an annual programme of courses run on a national basis by CIPFA and, in addition, many CIPFA regional organisations and audit groups run extremely cost-effective courses at a local level.

External training is generally more costly than in-service training, particularly where residential courses are used, and much care needs to be taken in selecting the right courses. However, topics are covered by external courses which could never be dealt with adequately on an in-service basis in all but the largest organisations. Some typical topics are as follows:

- Behavioural skills.
- Computer audit.
- Contract audit.

In addition, it is usually possible to attract a better range of expertise (in the form of experienced lecturers and practitioners) to externally organised courses, and facilities such as video equipment are often available.

One aspect of external training which is rarely used and has many advantages is secondment. Exchanges of staff between county/regional council and district councils, regional health authorities and district health authorities and their headquarters and regional offices, internal and external audit, government departments and local and health authorities, and even between public and private sector organisations, all have distinct possibilities. Those few public sector organisations that have tried this have reported advantages to the individual (from the point of view of personal development) and to the organisation (from the aspect of shared techniques, procedures and ideas).

Training records

Implicit in the development of a proper training programme is the maintenance of adequate training records for each member of staff. These are extremely useful in assessing further training needs and in comparing development between individuals. If an organisation has a training section, it will keep records as well as help organise the whole training programme.

CHAPTER 4

Audit planning and control

Paragraphs 45 and 46 of the APB *Guidance for Internal Auditors* lay great emphasis upon the importance of audit planning. They say that:

> Internal Audit work should be planned, controlled and recorded in order to determine priorities, establish and achieve objectives and ensure the effective and efficient use of audit resources.

Planning

The main purposes of internal audit planning are:

(a) to determine priorities and to establish the most cost-effective means of achieving audit objectives;
(b) to assist in the direction and control of audit work;
(c) to help ensure that attention is devoted to critical aspects of audit work; and
(d) to help ensure that work is completed in accordance with predetermined targets.

Preparing the plan

The audit manager should prepare strategic, periodic and operational work plans.

Strategic plan

The APB guideline suggests that the strategic plan will usually cover a period of two to five years during which time all major systems and areas of activity will be audited. The plan should set out the audit objectives, audit areas, type of activity, frequency of audit and an assessment of resources to be applied.

Strategic planning is by far the most important phase. This is an exercise in determining the broad objectives of the audit function and how those objectives will be achieved. In theory, little or no heed should be given, at this stage in the process, to the available manpower resources, but in practice some regard must be given to this if the strategic plan is to remain an achievable exercise. The following is a list of some of the more important questions which should be answered in the formulation of the strategic plan:

- What are the objectives of the audit function?
- How should the audit section be structured to achieve those objectives?
- Should there be audit teams? Should work be allocated on a subjective basis (e.g. payroll, creditors and contracts), an objective basis (i.e. services) or a geographical basis?
- Are any areas of activity to be omitted from the audit review?
- What is the minimum acceptable level of audit coverage?
- Are specialist skills needed (e.g. computer auditors)?
- Where are the auditors to be based (i.e. centrally or in divisional offices)?
- Is the audit approach to be system or regularity based?
- To what extent will the work of audit be co-ordinated with that of other review agencies (e.g. external audit, management services)?
- Does the auditor have any responsibility for the review of management information systems?
- Are any resources to be earmarked for value-for-money projects?

The APB guideline defines the stages of internal audit planning as:

1. Identifying the objectives of the organisation.
2. Defining internal audit's objectives.
3. Taking account of all relevant changes in legislation and other external factors.
4. Obtaining a comprehensive understanding of the organisation's systems, structure and operations.
5. Identifying, evaluating and ranking risks to which the organisation is exposed.
6. Taking account of changes in structures or major systems in the organisation.
7. Identifying audit areas by service, functions and major systems.
8. Determining the type of audit (e.g. systems, verification or value for money).
9. Taking account of the plans of external audit and other review agencies.
10. Assessing the staff resources required and matching them with the resources available.

The *objectives of the organisation* will need to be examined at different levels since each organisation is likely to have a mission statement or strategic plan which sets out the objectives for that body. There is also likely to be a senior management team which deals with strategic issues. Knowledge on these overall objectives will need to be added to by obtaining details of the objectives for each of the departments running the services and for any central services.

In *defining internal audit's objectives*, regard must be had to the APB guidelines and to any professional standards issued by other bodies.

To *take account of relevant legislation* there is a need to monitor both local and national press and the various information services available (e.g. material available from CIPFA including their periodical for members and the Financial Information Service; information from any organisations and associations connected with the organisation; and any relevant government circulars), so that the audit department is aware of the challenges which are facing their clients. In addition, procedures should be in place to ensure all proposed legislative changes are brought to audit's attention.

In order to gain a *comprehensive understanding of the organisation's systems*, there should be a continuous process for obtaining a picture of the structure and operations so that as each audit is undertaken information should be fed into the planning process to ensure that the plan remains relevant. As organisations are continually changing, audit knowledge should be up to date. It will be built upon the knowledge about the organisation as a whole.

Identifying, evaluating and ranking risks to which the organisation is exposed will flow out of the understanding of the organisation and knowledge of previous audits. There will be a need to *identify all systems* operating within the organisation, whether fundamental or minor, in order to know the full size of the audit area to be covered. Results of previous system reviews and how these areas are being covered in other audits across the organisation should be considered. The judgement arrived at, as a result of this consideration, should be documented and should lead to a joint plan for internal and external audit of the work to be performed.

Identifying audit areas by service, functions and major systems should flow out of regular meetings with senior staff in all departments and with the head of finance, to take account of their concerns. In addition to helping to keep the audit department up to date with an understanding of the organisation it also allows the managers to indicate any particular areas of weakness which are known to them which audit should review. When discussing the expectation of managers the opportunity should be taken to market the audit service to them and the results of all these discussions should also be fed into the planning process. The final plan should be one which, wherever possible, is owned by the department(s) being audited.

The audit manager must also determine the *type of audit* to be applied:

● A *systems audit* provides a detailed appraisal which helps to ensure that systems are efficiently designed, contain adequate internal control and produce sufficient and timely management information.

- A *value for money audit* involves reviews of a range of subjects across the breadth of the organisation's services and activities to consider efficiency, effectiveness and economy in the use of resources.
- A *verification audit* provides for routine visits to be made to establishments to assist management in maintaining high standards of financial management and administration.
- An *investigation audit* involves investigating and reporting upon all instances which may involve fraud, loss or irregularity; and any special investigation requested by management or by Financial Regulations.

In the same way as with management of the organisation, regular meetings should be held with *external audit*, management services' units or other corporate or departmental review bodies. Written minutes should be taken and commitment obtained to exchange plans.

Assessing the staff resources required and matching them with the resources available sounds a lot easier than it is in practice. A number of internal audit departments are restricted in the number of staff they have and make the best of those resources even though they know they need more. It is essential, however, to know the extent of any shortfall. To do this, audit must go through a proper planning process as outlined above which will result in a proper comparison between resources required and resources available. The audit manager should then take appropriate action to match the two sides, with the involvement of line management if necessary.

Periodic plan

Also referred to as the tactical plan, this will typically cover a financial or calendar year and translate the strategic plan into a schedule of audit assignments to be carried out in the ensuing period. It will define the purpose and duration of each audit assignment and allocate staff and other resources and should be formally approved by management.

This should enable each auditor to see the areas of activity they will be working on over the coming year. It can, however, be only a provisional allocation as plans need to be flexible to respond to changing priorities.

In devising the periodic plan, flexibility must be the keyword and the audit manager should not regard it as a sacrosanct expression of immutable audit policy. Put simply, the periodic plan assesses the workload imposed by the strategic plan and attempts to reconcile this with the resources available to carry out that work. It is, therefore, an exercise in balancing an equation – the *resources/workload* equation.

The first stage in balancing the equation is to determine the staffing resources that are available. This relatively straightforward task involves an assessment of the total work-days from which should be deducted the estimated days required to cover holidays, sickness, training and vacancies. It is important, for reasons which will become obvious later, that no allowance is made at this stage for any allocation of staff to 'non-audit' duties. Thus the *resources* side of the equation will take the following form:

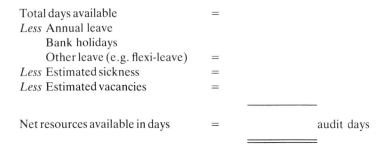

The second stage of the process is to assess the *workload*. This is the more complex side of the equation and entails a comprehensive review of all of the activities of the organisation. Having regard to the strategic plan, and the decisions taken therein, the audit manager must express each area of audit activity in the form of an audit day target. In so doing, the manager should not look at the available resources at this stage, but should consider the targets to be an expression of professional opinion as to the resources required to achieve the required level of audit coverage as stated in the strategic plan. In arriving at each target, the audit manager will have in mind such factors as:

- the resources required to conduct the audit in the past
- any history of unusual difficulties, such as frauds and irregularities
- the strength of the financial systems operating in the area and the extent to which audit will be able to rely upon them.

Many audit managers advocate the use of risk indices to allocate resources to individual audit tasks. These usually involve the calculation of aggregate income and expenditure figures, weighted by various risk factors, which are then used pro rata to determine the allocation of the available days. The assessment of risk does constitute an important part of the audit planning process and, at this stage in the development of the tactical plan, it is recommended that the audit manager should allocate a simple risk assessment to each audit task. Let us assume, for example, that the audit manager has decided to use a three-level risk index – high, average or low. The manager should then consider each audit task; and, having regard to a knowledge of the organisation and the varying risks associated with different kinds of income expenditure and assets, the manager should allocate one of the three risk factors to each task.

Frequency of audit plays an important part in the formulation of the tactical plan, and again the recommended approach is for the audit manager to allocate to each audit task the ideal frequency which professional experience suggests is necessary. It should then be possible to calculate the annual effect on days of each audit task and thereby the workload in terms of total days per annum. Thus the workload calculation will take the following form:

Audit task	Risk factor	Days required	Frequency	Annual effect
a	High	20	½ yearly	40
b	High	60	3 yearly	20
c	Average	10	Annually	10
d	Low	50	5 yearly	10
e	Average	10	Monthly	120
f	High	25	Annually	25
etc.	etc.	etc.	etc.	etc.
			Total days required	x

The two sides of the equation can now be compared. The possibility that the resources will exceed the workload is unlikely, and it is almost inevitable that the audit manager will be faced with reducing the workload somehow in order to balance it with the available resources. There are three basic choices open to the audit manager, as follows:

1. Omit certain tasks from the programme of work, possibly those designated as low risk.
2. Reduce the work-day allocation to individual audit tasks and thus carry out the audits in less depth.
3. Extend the frequency of the audits.

The likely outcome will be a combination of all three but, as a matter of principle, the third choice is favoured. Even low risk tasks, if they are left completely out of the programme, may eventually become high risks, and if the audit day allocation is reduced and only superficial reviews carried out, the whole audit process will be devalued. By far the best method of reducing the workload is to extend the frequencies of the 'low risk' tasks until they are regarded as 'average risk' and then, if necessary, to extend the frequencies of selected 'average risk' tasks until they become 'high risks'. In this way the periodical plan can be balanced.

Approval of the plan

We now reach a crucial stage in the planning process – the approval of the plan. It is a comparatively painless exercise for management to agree a strategic plan with the audit manager, as it involves decisions about audit policy without reference to available resources. It is not quite so painless, but none the less essential, for management to consider the operational plan. Bear in mind that this plan, as well as being a schedule of audit tasks to be completed, is also an expression of the risks which management is taking in providing fewer audit resources than are necessary to achieve the agreed strategy at the depth and frequency which the audit manager considers appropriate. Therefore it is important that the operational plan receives approval at that level of management which has the power to allocate, or at least to recommend the allocation of, additional staffing resources should it consider the risks to be too high. It is equally important that the plan should draw attention to those tasks which have had to be omitted and to the areas where input has been restricted or where frequencies have been extended in order to balance the equation.

Once the operational plan is agreed, the audit manager can move to the final stage of the planning cycle – the production of an operational plan.

Operational/work plans

These should be prepared for each audit assignment and include:

- objectives and scope of the audit;
- time budget and staff allocation; and
- methods, procedure and reporting arrangements, including supervision and allocation of responsibilities.

These should be communicated to the service head as the terms of reference for the audit, with a request for a named contact to start work. If correct procedures on consultation are in place there should not be long delays before actual work can start. In simple terms, the operational plan divides the tactical plan into manageable bites of usually not more than a few weeks' duration. In deciding which tasks to include in the operational plan, the audit manager will have regard to a number of factors, including the following:

- *Timing* The planned frequency of the task, and the elapsed time since it was last completed, must be considered.
- *Geographical location* It is often desirable and, indeed, more economical to undertake a number of audit tasks together in the same geographical vicinity.
- *Availability of special expertise* Some tasks may require an input from specialist staff and the availability of such staff will thus influence the operational plan.
- *Special events* It is sometimes advantageous to coincide audit visits with special events, such as payday, the month or year end, or at a time when income or expenditure is at its peak.
- *Seasonal factors* Many activities are seasonal and this may well have a

bearing upon the timing of an audit task; for example, there would be little use in conducting an audit of a grasscutting bonus scheme in the middle of winter!

- *Work patterns* There will be times when the auditor will be less welcome than usual because of workload peaks. Reviews of the budget preparation system, therefore, should not be scheduled at a time when the accountants are busy preparing estimates.
- *Information received* A 'tip-off', anonymous or otherwise, may well influence the audit manager to bring forward a particular audit task.

These are some of the more common factors and there will, no doubt, be many more. Once the operational plan has been fixed, the audit manager will communicate its contents to the audit staff in the form of work instructions. Arrangements will vary between organisations, but such instructions should always be in writing and should state, *inter alia*, the nature of the task, the staff to be involved, the time allocated to the task and details of the work to be carried out. It is likely that the written instructions to staff will include a detailed audit programme. (Audit programmes are dealt with in more detail in Chapter 5.)

The audit manager may separate value for money activities and systems review from the transaction-based activities, in which case individual value for money and systems review tasks will have been included in the tactical plan. Alternatively, each audit task may contain an element of systems and value for money reviews.

Whatever the detailed instructions contain, if the planning process is to be successful it will be necessary for the audit manager to employ an effective 'cut off'. In other words, the manager must be able, by various means, to maintain the schedule of audit tasks within the allotted time. However, if it becomes necessary to conclude an audit task before the scheduled work has been completed, it is essential that it is the less important aspects of the work which are omitted. A useful technique to ensure that this is achieved is to allocate a priority rating to each individual activity. Each activity is then completed in order of priority, thus leaving the least essential tasks to the end. In this way the important matters will be dealt with at each audit and, by rotating the less important tasks, they too will receive attention on a reasonably regular basis.

Many audit managers build into their tactical plans an element to cover contingencies, such as unplanned work (special investigations, frauds, etc.), and to extend target times when this is thought necessary. In this way, a more flexible approach to 'cut off' can be adopted. Others regard an inbuilt contingency as a resigned acceptance that the planned targets will never be achieved. To fail to recognise that unplanned work will arise and/or targets will have to be exceeded occasionally is unrealistic. Therefore, to omit a contingency element from the tactical plan is equally unrealistic.

Controlling the audit

Control of the internal audit department and of individual assignments is needed to ensure that internal audit objectives are achieved and work is performed effectively. The most important elements of control are the direction and supervision of the internal audit staff and review of their work. This will be assisted by an established audit approach and standard documentation. The degree of control and supervision required depends on the complexity of assignments and the experience and proficiency of the internal audit staff but by applying supervision the audit manager should help ensure the following:

1. Conformity exists with the standards and internal audit procedures laid down in the audit manual.
2. At the outset of an audit there is provision of suitable instructions to subordinates and approval of assignment plans.
3. Assignment plans are carried out, unless deviations are both justified and authorised.
4. Appropriate audit techniques are used.
5. Working papers support audit findings, conclusions and reports.
6. Audit reports are accurate, objective, clear, concise, constructive and timely.
7. Audit objectives are met within allocated time budgets, both actual and elapsed, unless there are valid reasons for change.
8. Working papers are being prepared to support internal audit findings and conclusions.
9. Internal audit's performance is in accordance with the internal audit plan or that any significant variations have been explained.

The audit manager should, therefore, establish arrangements:

- *to allocate audit assignments according to the level of and proficiency of audit staff.* Clearly there is a need for a judgement to be made, for each audit, as to the level of experience and skills required. At the two extremes there may be a complicated value for money review across the whole organisation or a simple petty cash review. These jobs will need to be matched to the appropriate member of staff. Procedures will need to be in place so that there is appropriate knowledge of the capabilities of each member of staff;
- *to ensure that auditors clearly understand their responsibilities and objectives.* The audit manager should specify the required standard of internal audit documentation and working papers and then ensure that those standards are maintained. This can best be reflected in an audit manual which should provide the main source of guidance on how working papers should be prepared;

- *to communicate the scope of the work to be performed and agree the programme of work with each internal auditor.* Each auditor should know, in general terms the assignments to be carried out during the year, although flexibility must be maintained. For each assignment the auditor must know the type of audit being undertaken (e.g. value for money or systems review), the start date, days available for the job, contact point, target date for completion and details of any other staff involved. Draft terms of reference should also be compiled either by the auditor or by a supervisor if the auditor is inexperienced. Ideally these terms of reference will be agreed with the client before the audit starts;
- *to provide and document evidence of adequate supervision, review and guidance during the internal audit assignment.* (This is discussed further in Chapter 5, Audit documentation.)

The objective of this monitoring stage is to assess the degree to which the plan has been achieved in practice. Audit plans should allocate time budgets to tasks and the audit manager should continually monitor performance against these budgets and thus be able to identify at an early stage if plans are not being met.

Most systems used for this purpose revolve around the completion of time sheets by audit staff to indicate how their time has been spent. Various types of computer software are available to support this task, the most commonly used being the spreadsheet. This allows details of targets and achievements to be recorded against individuals and then for various analyses to be performed to show individual and overall attainments of targets. The results can subsequently be displayed in graphic and pictorial form so that the progress of individual assignments is immediately visible.

To help exemplify the monitoring process, one relatively simple system, which has been found to work well in practice, is operated as follows:

1. An entry is maintained for each audit task on a spreadsheet. It shows the nature of the task, planned frequency, risk factor and the time target.
2. Time sheets are kept by audit staff, recording how their time has been allocated between audit tasks to the nearest quarter day.
3. Auditors are made aware of their targets, and that targets may not be exceeded without the permission of the audit manager.
4. Using the time sheets and a spreadsheet, team leaders can produce a monthly summary of staff time showing time spent on:
   - designated tasks;
   - work in excess of planned targets (contingency);
   - unplanned exercises (contingency);
   - training;
   - holidays;
   - sickness; and
   - vacancies.

5. The audit manager maintains a composite spreadsheet for all audit teams and compiles a consolidated spreadsheet at monthly intervals. Charts are produced which indicate, in graphic form, the planned cumulative target for each element of the plan. Monthly summaries are then plotted against the cumulative targets, thus providing a broad picture of performance.

Reviewing the plan

The final stage in the process is to use the information gained from the monitoring stage to review the success of the plan. This will be done informally after each operational plan and more formally before the production of a new tactical and/or strategic plan. In this way, successive audit plans will be built on experience and thus should be increasingly successful.

The objective is to compare actual time spent on various sections of the audit with that which was planned. Where the plan was clearly generous, it can be reduced accordingly and, where it proved to be inadequate, a decision can be taken as to whether the allocation should be increased for future periods or whether the programme of tests in that area should be modified to reduce the input. However, the review should not be restricted to a mathematical exercise. The opportunity should be taken at each review to re-examine the objectives of the audit and to consider whether the correct strategy is being used – in other words, to review the strategic and operational plans.

CHAPTER 5
Audit documentation

The APB guideline requires that there should be documentary evidence of adequate supervision, review and guidance during the internal audit assignment, and that adequate working papers should be prepared to support internal audit findings and conclusions.

In most disciplines, good documentation is almost as important as good practical work. In the field of audit, documentation assumes an even greater degree of importance. The most thorough of audits, if not supported by detailed, accurate and comprehensible documentation, is of little practical value. The very nature of audit work, often involving the criticism of the work of others, attracts challenge. Internal audit work should be properly recorded, therefore, because:

1. The audit manager needs to be able to ensure that work delegated to staff has been properly performed. This can generally be done only by reference to detailed working papers prepared by the internal audit staff who performed the work.
2. Working papers provide for future reference, evidence of work performed, details of problems encountered and conclusions drawn.
3. The preparation of working papers encourages each internal auditor to adopt a methodical approach to work.

The audit manager should specify the required standard of internal audit documentation and working papers and ensure that those standards are maintained. The audit manual should provide the main source of guidance on how working papers should be prepared. This will also enable adequate supervision and review to take place.

Audit programmes

Audit programmes are an important and extremely useful means of communicating instructions to audit staff, and provide an excellent basis for recording work done. At its simplest, an audit programme is a list of audit activities to be carried out. In effect, it is a further stage of detail from the operational plan. If the operational plan can be said to be an expression of the audit tasks to be completed over a period of days/weeks/months, then audit programmes record the detailed tests and checks to be undertaken in order to complete each task. In other words, they comprise a series of written instructions from the audit manager to audit staff, recorded in such a way as to constitute a programme of work to complete a particular audit task.

Opinion varies as to whether audit programmes should be extremely detailed, identifying every single activity required of the auditor, or whether they should provide only broad guidance as to the areas to be covered. Much depends upon the experience of the audit staff involved. Relatively new or inexperienced staff will need a more detailed audit programme to tell them precisely which tests and checks they are to carry out and the extent to which each test is to be conducted. On the other hand, more experienced staff need only broad guidance and, indeed, a detailed audit programme might generate an 'automatic' approach, thus stifling initiative.

Many publications already exist which provide examples of audit programmes to cover every conceivable aspect of audit work. It is not the intention to duplicate these here, but in order to illustrate audit programmes and to exemplify the extremes of detail which can be involved, some examples of such programmes have been included in Appendix 2.

Audit managers usually adopt the practice of cross-referencing audit programmes to systems records so that auditors can readily see how the compliance tests which they are conducting fit into the overall pattern of procedures. As the systems records will identify the weak points in internal control, this will also assist the auditor to concentrate on the tests covering these areas.

Chapter 4 mentioned the use of priority ratings as a means of effecting a 'cut off' to the audit whilst ensuring that the more important tasks are always carried out. The audit programme is a useful vehicle for expressing those priorities. Each item in the programme can be allocated a priority rating and those with a high priority may then be tackled first. In this way the audit can, if necessary, be concluded at an early stage, leaving only the low priority items uncompleted.

Working papers

One of the main purposes of audit working papers is to provide assurances that conclusions are soundly based. Consequently audit work must be documented at all levels so that any reviewer can follow the logical flow from strategic audit planning through to assignment completion and reporting. Working papers must provide, therefore, for evidence of:

- comprehensive audit planning;
- systems documentation and key control evaluation;
- specific assignment objectives;
- audit approach to each assignment (including terms of reference);
- information obtained;
- details of problems encountered;
- the results of work;
- validly based judgements and conclusions;
- testing, showing the objective, method, results and conclusions of each test; and
- review.

Working papers should always be sufficiently complete and detailed to enable an experienced auditor, with no previous connection with the audit assignment, subsequently to ascertain from them what work was performed and to support the conclusions reached. Working papers should be prepared as the internal audit assignment proceeds so that critical details are not omitted and problems not overlooked. These should be reviewed by internal audit management.

These procedures are required to ensure that the relevant guidance within the APB guideline referring to the evaluation of the internal control systems, due care and evidence are all complied with satisfactorily. All audit files, whether manual or computerised, should be retained for an appropriate period which could be as long as six years, and filed in a manner which ensures their safe custody and confidentiality.

To ensure clarity all working papers should at a minimum be properly indexed; cross-referenced to show the logic or trail of audit work; and marked, where appropriate, with their originating source.

Various types of audit working papers are in use and commonly these will include the following:

- *Standard working papers* These are cross-referenced, where appropriate to the audit report and other working documents.
- *Query sheets* These are lists of questions which arise during the audit, together with answers received. These should be cross-referenced to the standard working papers.
- *Lists of unsettled items* These are carried forward to the next audit, and are cross-referenced to the original standard working papers.
- *Audit summary sheets* These are often used by team leaders to summarise the main items arising from the audit.
- *An audit programme* This will often form a working paper itself, in as far as it may be used to record the extent of tests and checks undertaken.

It is an important facet of supervision that audit staff should be required to initial every working paper which they complete. Similarly, senior staff charged with reviewing the work should also be required to initial working papers, as this encourages a responsible attitude and enforces a supervisory discipline which might otherwise be lacking.

Many audit managers find it useful to devise standardised working papers as this assists them to locate easily the various component parts of the audit as they conduct their reviews. Wordprocessing facilities provide the auditor with the opportunity to devise 'templates' for various types of documentation so that standards can be devised and maintained. These standards may include such criteria, as:

1. Each working paper should be properly titled with the name of the audit, the date and the nature of the work recorded.
2. The audit file reference should be recorded, together with any cross-references to the audit programme, systems records and any associated working papers.
3. All working papers should be neat, legible and prepared with the same degree of care and attention as the audit report itself.

Perhaps the most effective test of the adequacy of a working paper is that, if it fell out of the audit file and was picked up by an informed stranger, then the person should be able to determine what it is, what it records, who had produced and checked it and in which file it belongs. How many working papers would pass such a test?

Audit files

Well-kept audit files are a sign of an efficient and well-managed audit section. An important part of preparing for an audit involves reviewing the previous year's audit, and this can be rendered difficult, if not impossible, by poor audit files. This is particularly so if the auditor is unfamiliar with the audit. In these circumstances, the auditor will need to place great reliance upon the existing audit files. Similarly, the audit report is built on the foundation of its supportive working papers and it is vital that these are filed in a manner which facilitates ease of information retrieval. As with working papers, standardised formats can be achieved through the use of wordprocessing software which can assist in enforcing standards on the one hand and also in filing and retrieving audit information on the other.

Audit files can be conveniently divided into two categories – *permanent information files* and *current files*. Permanent information files contain data which are needed at each audit. Examples are as follows:

1. Systems records and internal control questionnaires (ICQs).

2. Staffing structure.
3. Standing orders and financial regulations.
4. Accounting and other relevant instructions.
5. Audit programmes.
6. Salary, wages and bonus rates.

Current files, on the other hand, contain all of the working papers and reports relating to the current audit, including completed audit programmes and ICQs.

Permanent information files must be kept up to date and it is an important role of the audit manager to make sure that audit staff are kept supplied with the most up-to-date permanent information possible. It is impossible to generalise about the content of current audit files but, as a guide, they might contain the following:

1. Audit working papers cross-referenced to query sheets, 'next audit notes' and the audit report.
2. Audit query sheets cross-referenced to the audit report.
3. The completed audit programme, showing the work done and who did it, cross-referenced back to working papers and query sheets.
4. Completed systems' internal control questionnaires and other working papers.
5. The audit summary report cross-referenced to all of the above documents.
6. The final audit report, together with a copy of the supporting letter to management.
7. A record of management decisions and proposals arising from audit recommendations, indicating the date for implementation.
8. A list of matters carried forward to the next audit – 'next audit notes'.

It is important that auditors remember that audit files are high security records and that they often contain confidential, and even controversial information. Too often audit files are left unattended on desks at the audit location or are stored at headquarters in an insecure manner. 'On location' they should be under the supervision of senior audit staff at all times; in the audit office they should be locked in secure cabinets and made available only to authorised personnel. Where audit files are held in wordprocessed form then access to the computer and associated disks must be controlled.

Audit reports

The purpose of an audit report is to convey to the recipient the results of the audit and the problems and weaknesses that have been identified. Its objective is to persuade management to take remedial action. It is, in fact, the 'shop window' for the considerable and expensive audit work which has gone before.

Much excellent audit work can be wasted if the resulting audit reports are unprofessional and ineffective. Wordprocessing software provides an opportunity to produce high quality and well-presented reports. They provide, too, the added benefit of being able to include graphs and pictures from associated spreadsheet software to enhance the report and help make the overall arguments more convincing. A picture is worth 1000 words!

Where, in the midst of an audit, a serious problem is discovered which requires immediate attention, it may be necessary to issue an interim report; however, audit reports are normally produced at the end of the audit process. Generally speaking, at the end of an audit one of three situations will apply, as follows:

1. There may be no matters to be raised.
2. There may be only a few minor matters to be raised.
3. There may be major criticisms or so many minor matters as to constitute a major problem.

Where there are no matters to be raised the external auditor will have certification to fall back on as a natural conclusion to the audit. The internal auditor, however, is faced with the alternative of issuing a report (or a letter) which says that nothing amiss has been found, or of doing nothing and effectively leaving the audit in mid-air. If the latter course is adopted, the audit manager may miss a golden opportunity to create good working relationships; to dispel the view that auditors only criticise; and, more importantly, to applaud and encourage good internal control. At the same time, the line manager, who has suffered the inconvenience of the audit presence, is left wondering whether or not the audit has been concluded and whether the wrath of the chief executive is about to fall. Without doubt, the audit manager should ensure that the customer is left in no doubt about the outcome of the audit.

Where only a few minor criticisms emerge at the end of the audit, it is essential that these are not elevated to a position of over-importance by the manner in which they are reported. The report should be congratulatory and should simply make passing reference to a few minor issues which require attention and which are relegated to an appendix. In this way, the minor matters will receive attention, but the auditor's perspective and sense of proportion will be seen to be sound.

Finally, where major criticisms occur, or so many minor items are raised as to constitute a major problem overall, it will be necessary to prepare a 'full blown' audit report; the remainder of this section will deal with the production of that report.

The independence of the auditor dictates the right to report in his/her own name and without censorship on any aspect of the organisation. To justify this, the auditor must be able to produce a high quality professional report and must have clear reporting lines. There should be no restrictions imposed as to whom to report to and the auditor must have the recipient of the report clearly in mind at all times whilst preparing the document. The report must be written in such a way that the recipient will easily understand it; the objective is to communicate rather than to impress.

The report should be as concise as possible since the briefer it is, the more impact it is likely to have because busy line managers will then take the trouble to read it. It is always useful to summarise the main points contained in the report at the beginning, in order that senior management can assimilate the key issues quickly.

Jargon should be avoided at all costs, as should vague terms, such as 'a few', 'many' and 'a sample'. It is of little use to tell a line manager that a sample of transactions has been tested and a few have been found to be wrong. The manager needs to know how many have been tested, how many are wrong and in what way they are incorrect.

Finally, it is recommended that a 'due date for implementation' of agreed recommendations is incorporated in the report. In this way, management is more likely to take prompt action and the auditor will have a useful yardstick against which to measure management's response to the proposals made.

Systems approach

Most modern audit sections have adopted a systems-based approach to their audits in the belief that this represents a far more efficient and effective use of scarce and expensive audit resources. The systems approach encompasses the concept that prevention is better than cure. In such circumstances, the systems records maintained by audit assume prime importance. The techniques of systems audits will be discussed later, when the various records which are associated with the approach will be dealt with.

Systems records are 'permanent information' documents which, not surprisingly, form a record of the major systems of internal control. The purpose is to help the auditor to understand the systems fully, to assist in identifying weaknesses and key control features and to provide a permanent record upon which subsequent systems audits may be based.

Sources of information

It is important that management makes sure that the people for whom it has responsibility have the resources which they need to carry out their designated tasks. One of the main resources needed by an auditor is information; without this the auditor cannot function properly. It follows, therefore, that one of the fundamental duties of an audit manager is to ensure that the audit staff have as much information as possible at their disposal. This does not mean, of course, that the audit section should have a vast library. It simply means that auditors should be made aware of the information that is available and where it can be obtained. It is not necessary, for example, for the audit department to keep copies of every statute, but auditors should be kept informed of those which are relevant to their duties and where they may be seen.

The information required by auditors can conveniently be divided into three broad categories, as follows:

- *Permanent information* This information is needed at all audits.
- *Temporary information* This information is needed only at one particular audit.
- *Operational information* This is information which is obtained in the course of the audit.

The responsibility for obtaining *operational* information obviously rests with the auditor, and the audit manager's role lies in ensuring that *permanent* and *temporary* information sources are comprehensive and up to date.

Permanent information

Permanent information will include the following items:

1. Statutes.
2. Statutory instruments.
3. Circulars (government and other).
4. Guidance from CIPFA and other professional bodies.
5. Comparative statistics from various sources.
6. Technical reference books.
7. Professional magazines and publications.
8. Standing orders, financial regulations, accounting manuals and various memoranda of accounting instructions.
9. The minutes of the organisation.
10. A chart showing staffing structures with positions and grades.
11. A list of establishments and locations.
12. A list of officers authorised to place orders, together with any limitations (e.g. 'food only' or 'goods/services below £1,000').
13. A list of officers authorised to certify invoices for payment, together with any constraints.
14. Descriptions in either narrative or flowchart form of all major systems of internal control.

Temporary information

The following are some examples of temporary information:

1. Recent officer reports to members of the board.
2. A current staff list.
3. A list of present pay points.
4. A current price list and approved charges.
5. Recent computer exception reports.
6. Relevant newspaper cuttings.

Operational information

It is not possible to produce a comprehensive list of examples of operational information because of the wide range of such information that is required by an audit section. Suffice it to say that this information is directly linked to the specific requirements of individual audits. This will include samples of various transactions (e.g. invoices, orders, inventory items and payments to employees over 65) which will be used in the course of the audit.

CHAPTER 6
Conducting an audit

We have dealt so far with the necessity to set objectives, determine management procedures and set down the ground rules for documenting the audit. In this chapter the practical issues of conducting an audit will be discussed and these include the necessary preparatory work, the practical aspects of conducting systems and regularity audits, and the reporting lines and the range of options which are, or at least should be, open to the audit manager.

Preparation for an audit

Staff should never arrive at an audit location unprepared for the task. This results in a waste of the auditor's and the auditee's time and it is damaging to the efficient image of audit. However good the relationship between the auditor and the auditee may be, there is bound to be resentment over the time the auditee has to spend in providing information and explanations. If this time can be kept to a minimum, and if the auditor has done a reasonable amount of advance preparation, then much will have been done to maintain good working relationships.

Advance notice

An important question to be answered at the preparation stage is whether advance notice of audit should be given to the auditee. Much depends upon the nature of the audit; for example, it would not be appropriate to give advance notice of a spot check on cash holdings or of a visit to investigate a suspected fraud. Generally, however, advance notice should be given. It would be totally unfair to expect an auditee, without advance warning, to rearrange a schedule in order to accommodate an audit visit. If, however, notice is given then the auditee can make sure that all records are available and that every member of staff who is needed is present. This can avoid much wasted time on both sides. Too much notice should not be given, however, as this would allow incomplete records to be brought up to date and errors and omissions to be rectified. A happy medium would be one to two days' notice.

Previous audits

Much can be gained from reading audit files: items brought forward for action at this visit and areas of past difficulty can be noted; a 'feel' of the audit can be gained; and a general picture can be built up of the efficiency of the organisation to be audited.

Audit programmes

The audit programmes to be completed should be obtained and studied. Any additional work to be done should be agreed upon and priorities should be established in order that the most important tasks are completed first. Thus, if the audit has to be concluded before all items have been covered, at least the major matters will have been dealt with. It should be stressed that the high priority items may include checks which, in isolation, may not appear to be important but, because they have been omitted for a number of audits, have assumed a higher level of priority.

Systems

From the systems records the auditor should become familiar with the major systems of financial control. Certainly these records will be available at the audit location, but there is nothing more annoying to an auditee than an auditor who continually has to stop to consult his records, thus demonstrating his lack of knowledge and preparation.

Personnel

This may seem a fairly simple point, but auditors should not arrive at the audit location not knowing the names of the officer in charge and the senior staff with whom they must deal. A good auditor will also have found out about the personalities of the key members of staff and even their hobbies and interests. In this way a useful 'ice-breaking' conversation can be readily initiated.

Protocol

Allied to the need to know the names of key personnel is the need to observe protocol and this may well vary from department to department. Many chief officers have quite strong views about who should be consulted at the beginning and end of an audit and throughout its course. In the absence of any stated rules of protocol, it is suggested, as a general principle, that no work should be done in a department without the chief officer (or their nominee) being informed beforehand and, at the commencement of a visit to an outstation (for example, a transport depot or stores), the auditor should first report to the person in charge. Similarly, it is courteous to report again at the end of an audit visit – if for no other reason – to thank the person in charge for their cooperation and to discuss the more important matters that have arisen.

Pre-selection of data

Much work needs to be done in advance of the audit in preselecting various items of information which will be used. Examples of paid invoices may be selected for checking against goods received, stores or inventory records, or for a physical verification of work completed. Lists of controlled stationery issued to the establishment may need to be prepared for eventual verification at the audit. Computer retrieval software may need to be run to provide details of various matters, such as numbers and grades of employees, overtime paid, analysis of expenditure over individual creditors, outstanding debtors over three months old, etc.

Selection of staff

The right blend of audit personnel needs to be achieved. Regard should be given to the complexity and importance of the audit, the volume of work to be completed and any special operations required. The audit manager should also consider the personality of the auditee and thus the behavioural qualities needed by the auditor. In this way a balanced team can be organised which will be best suited to the task in hand.

Systems audit

As mentioned in Chapter 5, the trend in audit is towards a systems-based approach. This is not to say that the regularity audit is unnecessary – indeed, the next part of this chapter is devoted to it – but that prevention is better than cure. Thus the establishment of secure and efficient systems of control is of paramount importance. It is necessary to recognise, however, that the establishment of such systems is management's task, not internal audit's. Often audit is seen as the 'systems design team'. The danger here is that it would be particularly difficult for audit to adopt a totally independent position if it were required to review a system which it had designed itself. In addition, it is unlikely that management would adopt with any enthusiasm a system which had been imposed upon them. Such a system would always be regarded as 'audit's system' and the tendency would be to allow it to flounder or even to sabotage it.

There are certain distinct stages in a systems audit and the remainder of this section will discuss the practical implications of these in the following order:

1. Identifying the major financial systems.
2. Recording the systems.
3. Testing the systems.
4. Reviewing the controls and identifying the weaknesses.
5. Eliciting improvements.
6. Compliance testing and reviewing.

There is one golden rule that every auditor should bear in mind when reviewing systems – no control should cost more than the likely loss if that control did not exist. In other words, in recommending improvements in systems, the auditor should have regard to the economy of controls. It is too often the case that auditors try to produce the 'perfect system' by means of elaborate and costly procedures which simply cannot be justified.

Identifying the major financial systems

There can be no hard and fast rules on this. What is a major financial system in one organisation may not be so in another. However, in general terms, a major financial system will control a significant part of the income, expenditure or asset holdings of the organisation. These generally will include the following:

1. Payroll systems.
2. The payment of creditors.
3. Debtors.
4. A cash income system.
5. Postal remittance systems.
6. Stocks and stores systems.
7. Inventory systems.
8. A terrier of property.
9. Loans and borrowing.
10. Investments.
11. Cash security.
12. Bank reconciliation.
13. Controlled stationery.
14. Petty cash expenditure.
15. Procedure for preparation of budget.
16. Budgetary control.
17. Project appraisal.
18. Control of manpower.
19. Capital expenditure controls.
20. Pension benefits.

Recording the systems

As already discussed, systems records can be in either narrative or flowchart form (or possibly a combination of both). Narrative format has the advantage of being easy to understand but it is too easy to gloss over complications. The completion of a flowchart imposes the discipline of following every stage of the system to its absolute conclusion. To a trained eye, a flowchart is more readily understood and a particular activity can quickly be traced through the system. Many flowchart formats are available and they all achieve much the same objective – to provide a visual record of the system in operation.

Testing the systems

At this stage the systems will probably have been recorded on the basis of a verbal description provided by management. Unfortunately, the tendency is to describe the systems as they should operate, rather than how they actually operate in practice. It is only human nature to cut corners, but often this will obviate controls which have been built into systems. To overcome this, it is necessary, having recorded the systems, to select a sample of transactions and to 'walk them through' the systems. In this way any departures can be identified and recorded. Thus an accurate picture can be obtained of how the systems work in practice.

Reviewing the controls and identifying the weaknesses

The next stage in the exercise is to review the controls; that is, to find out whether internal check and other control factors exist. It is also important to identify any weaknesses in controls in the form of an absence of internal check and other control factors. At the same time, it may be possible to locate inefficient or unnecessary procedures.

Eliciting improvements

Where control weakness and inefficient or unnecessary procedures have been identified, these should be drawn to management's attention and recommended improvements should be requested. Management can be guided as to the sort of improvements which are necessary, but the audit section should not be seen to be redesigning the whole system. The possibility exists, of course, that management may refuse to make any changes to the system, claiming that it is fine as it is. There are various methods of dealing with situations such as this. One thing that an auditor can do is to write to the line manager, recording the criticisms and stating that the line manager has the ultimate responsibility and will, no doubt, be prepared to be totally accountable for any problems which might arise from the weaknesses which have been identified in the systems. This approach usually has the desired effect.

Compliance testing and reviewing

It is necessary, at regular intervals, to test compliance with the agreed system, particularly with the key control features. Internal control questionnaires specially designed for the system are a useful means of achieving this. It is also important, from time to time, to review the system in the light of changing circumstances to make sure that the controls continue to be relevant and up to date.

Regularity audit

Regularity auditing is that part of the audit which tests by means of sampling transactions, that the 'rules' of the organisation have been adhered to, that material fraud and significant levels of error are not in evidence and that the organisation is acting within its statutory powers.

In practice it is impossible to divorce the systems audit from regularity audit and, for that matter, from value for money reviews. They are all part of the same process. However, in the interests of simplicity, each part is dealt with separately – value for money is covered in Chapter 11.

The extent of the regularity audit will be influenced by the results of the systems audit. Thus, in an area where systems are strong and are adhered to in practice, the regularity audit can be reduced. Conversely, where procedures are weak and little confidence can be placed in controls, then a more extensive regularity audit will be necessary.

Regularity audit is usually organised on the basis of audit programmes which do the following:

1. They test the various rules, both internal and external, that have been set up to see that the activities of the organisation have complied with them and that, consequently, the income and expenditure of the organisation have been handled properly, the assets have been kept secure and the various financial transactions have been recorded properly. These rules will include standing orders, financial regulations, accounting manuals and instructions, inventory regulations, stock control procedures, etc.
2. They test that no significant levels of error occur.
3. They test that there are no significant frauds and other irregularities.
4. They test that, where appropriate, there are no *ultra vires* transactions and thus that the activities of the organisation fall within its statutory powers.

Regularity audit is regarded by many as the bread and butter of an auditor's work and it does in many respects represent the layman's view of the role of the auditor. However, it is important to ensure that this somewhat mundane image of regularity audit does not lead to a robotic approach. Regularity audit requires flair and imagination if it is to achieve anything.

The art of sampling pervades most aspects of audit work, but perhaps none more so than regularity audit. Sampling, statistical or otherwise, is a wide-ranging subject about which many books have been written, so it is not the intention to deal with it here in any detail. Opinions vary amongst auditors as to the benefits of sampling. Some auditors regard scientific sampling as being of little value, whilst others advocate a comprehensive statistical approach to the selection of audit samples and the interpretation of their results.

Statistical sampling is particularly useful in error-testing large volumes of transactions. Using various statistical tests one can determine, to high levels of confidence, the likely degree of error, whilst checking relatively few transactions. Statistical sampling routines are increasingly available in retrieval software packages and there are also purpose-written statistical sampling software packages which can provide sophisticated sampling facilities for the auditor. Many auditors find random number tables a useful means of selecting samples. Stratified sampling enables the auditor to form an opinion about various sizes of transaction; for example, the selection and checking of samples of contracts from various value bands can help to evaluate the degree of control existing in those bands. This may, for example, lead to the conclusion that there is less control on contracts below £10,000 and, indeed, more losses occurring at that level. Without stratified sampling, the auditor would inevitably concentrate more time on high value contracts.

The biased approach to sampling – the selection of the obvious error/irregularity – is more pragmatic. Providing that one is not seeking to form an opinion about a large volume of transactions, this approach does serve wonderfully to focus audit attention on areas where it is most likely to be productive and, indeed, where it is likely to have the greatest impact in terms of results and publicity.

For all its unglamorous image, regularity audit can produce dramatic results. Many managers have been persuaded to improve systems controls, not because of a major review of the system, but because imaginative regularity tests have proved that the control weaknesses have actually resulted in errors or irregularities of material proportions.

Reporting lines

The independence of the audit manager and the importance of the freedom to report in an unrestricted fashion to any level in the organisation, upon any topic, have already been discussed. Here, these concepts will be expanded upon and reporting lines in general will be covered.

Reporting lines can be either formal or informal and it is important to stress that it is the authors' view that formal reporting lines should be established at the start, committed to writing and communicated to all relevant levels in the organisation. This can do much to avoid misunderstandings and disagreements.

It should be established to whom the audit manager reports in an administrative sense and, in many organisations, this will usually be the head of finance. Different arrangements exist in other organisations, with audit managers reporting to, for example, the management board. What is essential is that this reporting line in no way detracts from the auditor's independence and under no circumstances inhibits the freedom to report. A prime example of an administrative reporting line which would be inhibitive is an audit manager who reports to an assistant director of finance who also has responsibilities for certain line functions.

It also needs to be established to whom an audit manager reports in a professional sense on the following items:

1. Planning and progress.
2. General issues of financial control.
3. The results of specific audit exercises.
4. Fraud, corruption or other discovered irregularities.
5. Issues of value for money.

Reports on planning and progress will normally be submitted to the officer to whom the audit manager is administratively responsible. Similarly, with reports on general financial control which give a overall picture of various departments, it can be of immense value if a report on these topics (perhaps in summary form) is also submitted to the chief executive. It is perhaps with the chief executive that an informal reporting line can be of most value.

The results of particular audit exercises should generally be destined for the officer who will have to put right any problems or weaknesses. This may well range from a 'middle manager' to a 'chief officer', depending upon the nature of the report and the seriousness of the weaknesses. A useful arrangement which works well in practice is for such reports always to go to the middle manager (e.g. head teacher, nursing sister, works manager, etc.) with a copy to the chief officer (e.g. director of education, director of public health, general manager, etc.). This arrangement should apply whether the report contains criticisms or merely records that all is well. The practice of informing the chief officer only when something is wrong is not to be encouraged. It is as useful for a chief officer to know which of the sections/establishments are running well as to know which are causing problems. However, where a report is seriously critical of the middle manager, it would be wise to direct this only to the chief officer who may take positive remedial action. Audit reports should always state the names of all persons to whom they have been sent.

A separate arrangement should exist for reports on frauds and irregularities and, again, it is important that this is formalised and fully understood by everyone. Line managers should be required to report immediately to the audit manager whenever any irregularity is suspected. The person to whom the audit manager reports at the conclusion of the investigation will vary considerably.

Generally, an audit manager will be expected to submit a report on a serious irregularity to the following:

1. The officer to whom he/she reports administratively (say, the director of finance).
2. The chief executive.
3. The chief officer concerned.

Some audit managers will report directly to the police without consultation and others will be constrained by elaborate reporting and consultation processes.

Reporting lines on value for money reports are relatively easy to establish. Clearly, the prime responsibility for value for money lies with line management. It follows, therefore, that any recommendations to improve value for money should be channelled to the chief officer in charge of the service concerned. To encourage positive thought and positive action, it is often useful to provide a copy for the chief executive.

One area fraught with difficulties involves reporting lines to elected and board members. Opinions range from the 'tell them nothing' stance to the view that members should be kept fully informed of internal audit activity. As is so often the case, it is a matter of individual judgement as to the likely effect. Certainly it is not suggested that all detailed audit reports should be channelled to members, but there can be distinct advantages in submitting regular progress reports, general reports upon standards of financial control and specific value for money reports at quarterly intervals or half-yearly or annually, perhaps through an appropriate committee such as a specially created audit committee.

Audit committees

Audit committees are not as well established in the public sector as they appear to be in the private sector though increasingly pressure is being exerted upon board and elected members to recognise the importance of establishing a direct communications with the audit department. The Higher Education Funding Committee, for example, requires colleges of higher education to establish audit committees.

CHAPTER 7
Audit testing and techniques

The APB guideline says that as part of the planning process the internal auditor should identify the whole range of systems within the organisation and should establish appropriate criteria to determine whether the controls are adequate and assist in achieving the objectives of the system. There are various testing procedures and techniques which an auditor can employ as part of the audit process and this chapter describes briefly some of the more popular methods.

Systems-based auditing

A systems-based approach enables the auditor to assess how well the internal controls of a system operate. The APB guideline identifies the stages of a systems audit as:

- identifying the systems parameters;
- determining the control objectives;
- identifying the expected controls to meet the control objectives;
- reviewing the system against the expected controls;
- appraising the controls designed into the system against control objectives;
- testing the actual controls for effectiveness against control objectives;
- testing the operation of controls in practice; and
- reporting on whether the system provides an adequate basis for effective control and whether it is properly operated in practice.

This approach helps ensure a systematic approach to auditing and the discipline of using such a methodology helps the auditor to demonstrate that the audit has been conducted against a recognisable standard.

Selecting the system for review may be influenced by a number of factors. Certain systems will be regarded as fundamental to the operation of the organisation and require close audit attention. Others may be less significant and require only occasional review. The auditor needs to assess the risks inherent in all systems and then determine which deserve attention. This review would have been conducted at the planning of the audit (see Chapter 4).

Identifying and evaluating controls

Identifying the control mechanisms in systems may be quite straightforward in a simple system but may involve substantial effort in a more complex system, particularly if it is computerised. The auditor needs to be equipped with the right tools to help identify and evaluate the controls but while some techniques are designed to record the control procedures, others more usefully provide a means of evaluating them. This does, however, present something of a dilemma for audit management. How far should the auditor's work be prescribed and how far it should be left to the judgement of the individual to record and evaluate systems? While professional judgement is critical to the success of any audit, there is nevertheless a benefit to the audit service within an organisation for a disciplined approach which enables all to understand the audit approach. This does not preclude the judgement of the audit but helps focus it on those areas which contribute to the delivery of the audit objectives. In deciding which recording and evaluation techniques to apply, therefore, the audit manager should weigh up the relative merits of the more popular methods.

Narrative recording

Narrative recording involves committing the system to paper in the form of the written word. It has the advantage of being simple and requires little formal training – except perhaps, in the use of wordprocessing software. It is easily understood by the layperson and it is relatively easy for a new auditor to come to grips with the system quickly. However, each individual has a unique style of expression which lends itself readily to misunderstanding and it is comparatively easy to 'gloss over' complications in a system using the narrative style. While wordprocessing techniques can be used to influence the style and format of such a method of recording, it tends to be the least effective method.

Flowcharts

Flowcharts provide a means of showing diagramatically the mechanics of a system of document flow. They require a certain level of acquired skill which involves training. Flowcharting software is available to help in constructing the chart and some of the packages are relatively easy to use. The flowcharts may not always be easily understood by the uninitiated and it can often take a long time to comprehend a system fully. However, they are rarely ambiguous and they have the considerable advantage of imposing the discipline of tracing every single aspect of a system to its ultimate conclusion. It is not possible to 'gloss over' complications in a flowchart without making a deliberately false record.

If well drawn, they can provide a valuable visual representation of the system, though care must be exercised to record only those processes which impact upon the control philosophy otherwise recording all the document flows in a complex system is likely to make the flowchart difficult to comprehend. Nevertheless the flowchart does provide a concise way of recording a system in detail; it provides a positive aid in identifying the adequacy of a system's security and controls; and (where there has been no change in the system) it is particularly valuable at subsequent audits in enabling other auditors to understand the document flows and the key control points.

Perhaps the most successful method of recording systems involves a combination of both narrative and flowchart styles. The flow of documents is recorded in the normal flowchart manner, but key operations are cross-referenced to a narrative description which provides a far more flexible and descriptive style.

The identification of weaknesses, and the amendments to systems agreed subsequently with management to obviate these, will be recorded in the normal audit report and resulting correspondence, as will the subsequent checks to test compliance of the amendments with the existing system. It is important to stress that systems records, to be of benefit, must be kept completely up to date. Hence it is vital that audit is notified immediately of any changes to the systems so that the records can be amended and the system reassessed.

Internal control questionnaires

An internal control questionnaire (ICQ) is a comprehensive checklist used on site by the auditor to discover and test internal control at an early stage in the review of an organisation or system. If well designed, it should enable the auditor to get a clear picture of the adequacy of the control points in the system under review. ICQs are usually designed as a series of logical questions which require the auditor to answer YES or NO with unsatisfactory answers usually requiring a NO answer. The questions are designed to probe key areas of internal control and are intended to assist the auditor to review internal controls. However, an auditor should not rely solely upon the answers given to an ICQ as the means of reviewing internal controls. ICQs need to be supplemented by compliance tests to ensure that theory and practice accord with each other. (Appendix 3 provides some examples of ICQs.)

The advantages of an ICQ are:

1. They provide a logical sequence of key questions thus ensuring a disciplined and comprehensive cover of the area under audit.

2. Potential weaknesses can be quickly highlighted.
3. Completion is straightforward and can be undertaken by junior staff.
4. They can be used alongside flowcharts and checklists to provide a good basis for testing.

There are some disadvantages:

1. They can inhibit further questioning if the auditor limits the discussion to the specific questions in the ICQ.
2. They can be too detailed and prescriptive.

Much depends upon the quality of the construction of the ICQ. A well-constructed ICQ will retain the focus on the key controls and be structured in a logical fashion which is comprehensive but not ambiguous.

Control matrices

Control matrices are a derivation of ICQs but demand more judgement by the auditor. The key control objectives are identified for the system under review (and typically this may consist of no more than six questions). Then for each key control objective a series of expected controls is identified. The auditor in reviewing the system will then form a view on the adequacy of the expected controls and determine whether the key control objective has been satisfied.

The advantage of this approach is that the auditor can exercise judgement in undertaking the review but the primary audit objectives are nevertheless well defined beforehand.

Audit programmes

An audit programme is a defined set of tasks which must be performed for any given audit. They provide a clear statement of the individual tasks which must be accomplished by the auditor and are best suited for inexperienced staff who are unfamiliar with the particular audit task they have been assigned. They are often used, therefore, as a training medium and examples of audit programmes are included in Appendix 2.

Testing systems

Audit tests can be categorised under three broad headings: *compliance tests*, *substantive tests* and *walk-through tests*.

Compliance tests

The objective of a compliance test is to gain assurance as to whether controls have operated effectively throughout the period concerned. They are designed to provide audit evidence that control procedures are being applied as prescribed. They are not intended to establish correctness or identify errors and if errors are found then the auditor should be concerned with the impact upon the effectiveness of the system being audited rather than upon the error itself. Quite simply then, compliance tests are intended to prove that the control procedures are working.

There are four main categories of compliance tests:

1. Examining documentary evidence of the operation of controls.
2. Re-performing a sample of transactions.
3. Observing control operations or interviewing staff to assess whether control tasks are being performed (though this tests a situation at only one point in time).
4. Passing test data through systems to test the controls.

Substantive tests

Substantive tests are tests of transactions and balances which seek to provide audit evidence as to the completeness, accuracy and validity of the information contained in the system records. They aim to verify the authenticity of the output itself and only indirectly test the adequacy of the control procedures. Substantive testing of balances is usually carried out to test the population on which it is required to give an opinion and to test specific areas of concern (where controls are known to be weak).

Walk-through tests

Walk-through tests follow a transaction or transactions through the system in order to see that the system description is correct and that no important features have been overlooked.

Statistical sampling

Statistical sampling helps provide the auditor with a more scientific approach to selecting data for review and for testing. It is critical that the auditor is quite clear why the test has to be applied and understands the scale of the overall population to be reviewed so that the correct testing approach is adopted.

Different sampling techniques can be applied: random number sampling, interval sampling, stratified sampling and cluster sampling, for example. Some audit retrieval software includes sampling criteria to enable the auditor to extract data from computerised files.

Computer-assisted audit techniques

This technique gives auditors an important independent access to auditable information which, in many instances, will be the main accounting records of the organisation. While initially data retrieval software was developed for mainframe computers, there is now an increasing availability of such products designed for the micro. One of the more widely used in the public sector is IDEA, a product developed specifically for auditors.

The advantages claimed for general purpose retrieval software are:

1. Opportunity for 100% review of data, thus overcoming limitations of a test audit.
2. Speed in processing.
3. Accuracy of processing, subject to the correct specification of parameters by the auditor.
4. More effective (and satisfactory) use of audit time in analysing the results of retrieval in place of manual extraction and checking of information.
5. More complete audit possible, using results in conjunction with test data and other techniques.
6. Independent access to data.
7. Relative ease of use.

Against these benefits it may be claimed that:

1. There are the costs of the package (or packages) and of the training required.
2. Inexperienced users of the package and of the systems being interrogated may produce inaccurate results.
3. It does not on its own necessarily give positive evidence of the working of controls, as it is an examination of processed data and cannot give information about controls not actually used.

CHAPTER 8
Computer audit

Computer audit principles are no different from those which operate in all other spheres of audit but the technical qualities of computers and their associated software make the application of audit objectives more difficult to appreciate and to apply. Over the past decade there has been a significant change in the range of products, speed of operation and complexity of the facilities provided by the Information Technology (IT) industry. IT has become central to the effective and efficient provision of services within the public and private sectors and few organisations can now survive without recourse to the technology.

Auditing in a computerised environment is now the norm and, while certain specialist skills are necessary when auditing in such circumstances, not all of the work demands a significant degree of computer knowledge. Indeed the spread of IT within an organisation may well mean that reliance on one or more computer audit specialists is no longer practical and that all auditors require to be trained in basic computer audit skills.

All auditors must be aware of the scope of IT within their organisation and how it is structured and managed. Organisations are likely to be exploiting a combination of mainframe, mini and micros to provide for the overall needs of their departments. In most organisations the trend will be for IT to be decentralised and so no longer can auditors concern themselves solely with the identifiable computer department: in many instances they will need to consider the use of computing facilities as a whole throughout the organisation, doubtless provided by local and wide area networks and possibly managed by an external contractor.

Computer audit coverage

Where an organisation uses computer facilities, the auditor has three broad areas to consider: those aspects relating to the management of the IT facilities;

those concerning the overall control of those services; and those relating to each individual application which makes use of those facilities. The last two areas are inter-dependent and the auditor will refer to both the general and the specific whichever aspect of computing is being audited.

The topics which the auditor needs to address, therefore, include:

1. *Management issues:*
   - the definition of the organisation's information and IT strategies;
   - the arrangements for acquiring IT facilities;
   - the policy for the costing of and charging for IT facilities;
   - the process for measuring the performance of the IT service; and
   - the procedures for identifying and developing new systems.
2. *General security:*
   - the security of all the IT facilities throughout the organisation – central, departmental and local.
3. *Individual applications:*
   - the controls governing the day-to-day functioning of each individual system – financial and non-financial – processed by computer.

Management issues

Reviewing management issues involves the following:

1. Identifying the presence of an IT strategy and the overall arrangements within the organisation for matching business needs with IT facilities.
2. Reviewing the structure and position of the IT department within the organisation.
3. Reviewing the processes for acquiring IT facilities.
4. Identifying the arrangements for the costing of computing facilities and for charging the users of those facilities.
5. Reviewing the arrangements for measuring the performance of the IT facilities.
6. Reviewing the arrangements for identifying the need for and arranging the development of new systems.

Strategy

In reviewing the IT strategy, the auditor should be concerned that a corporate computing strategy has been defined and adequate arrangements exist for its implementation and review. The auditor will be concerned, therefore, with whether a strategy exists, its method of formulation, and its scope and impact. As for its implementation and review, the auditor will need to review the procedures for its management, implementation and revision, and this will involve identifying the role of elected and board members and of senior management.

The appropriateness of the IT strategy in relation to the overall business strategy is critical. The auditor will therefore need to consider the link with a corporate strategy and whether it reflects all departmental requirements.

Acquisition

Since proper assessment of requirements is crucial to any successful acquisition of facilities, the auditor will need to review the analysis and decision-making process. With some exceptions, the procedures for acquiring IT facilities in the public sector must conform to detailed requirements laid down by European Commission directives. The auditor must be familiar with the legislation and ensure that those responsible for procurement conform to the rules.

Structure

The position of the computer department, its structure and its detailed organisation are all vital to the provision of effective computing. The auditor will therefore need to review the status of the computer department and assess whether the potential of computing is recognised. There should be a clear definition of responsibilities and of the structure and chain of command, and adequate consideration by management of staff issues such as recruitment, training, motivation and remuneration.

Costing

The auditor should assess whether the total costs of computing are identifiable and are effectively controlled and allocated. Central and user costs should be identifiable and a cost centre approach adopted to identify more readily the elements of costs. As for charging the users of services, the auditor should establish the basis of charges and the policy for recouping costs.

System development control

It is important that the auditor should be able to assure management that the development procedures are adequate and are applied in every situation, and that the organisation is efficiently developing those systems approved by an appropriate level of management after the consideration of all the relevant facts.

The overall objective of an audit review of these controls is to determine whether there are adequate procedures to ensure that the development and maintenance of systems within the organisation results in well-documented computer systems, incorporating adequate controls and meeting properly defined user requirements in an efficient manner.

The results and conclusions drawn from any review of the systems development and maintenance controls, will be very relevant to any work done in the review of individual systems. Where control over development is felt to be inadequate, and remedial action is not forthcoming, the auditor may well be best advised to spend a higher proportion of the time available in the review of the controls within individual computer systems.

These objectives will be satisfied by reviewing the following processes:

- *Planning* Are the long- and short-term system development proposals well defined?
- *Approval* Who takes decisions for approving developments?
- *Project planning* Is there an effective method of planning the entire development project?
- *Standards* Are system development standards used and adhered to?
- *User involvement* Does the user (the customer) get the opportunity to say what they want?
- *Post-implementation review* Is there some mechanism for comparing what was promised with what was delivered? Do the two coincide?
- *Maintenance* Are there effective arrangements for dealing with maintenance and for measuring the extent of such changes?

Computing resources

The performance of computing resources should be reviewed regularly by management with a view to optimising the continued efficiency and effectiveness of the resources. Many aspects of performance measurement are technical in nature but audit's role is to satisfy itself that the mechanisms are in place for the conduct of such reviews and for reporting the results to management.

Security issues

The auditor's task is to review the adequacy of the controls and procedures governing the organisation of staff, operational functions, access to files and software, terminal activity and general environmental protection to ensure that they provide secure, effective and efficient day-to-day operation of the computer installation.

When reviewing these procedures the auditor will need to pay close attention to organisational, operational, file and network controls.

Organisational controls

These are issues dealing with the organisation of the responsibilities of all staff involved in the computer process and the standards established for their efficient working. Here, the auditor will need to bear in mind that computing facilities will be spread throughout the organisation and so a key step will be to try to identify the areas most deserving attention.

Operational controls

These are issues relating to all aspects of the data preparation, data control and operating functions. This will include the day-to-day procedures for getting data into the computer process and ensuring that only authorised work is processed.

File controls

Controlling access to files and software, including the custody of physical magnetic files, will be a critical activity since this is the nub of the computer process and the area where one of the key assets of the organisation – its information – demands protection and safekeeping.

Network controls

With screens on desks being commonplace, these terminals and micros connected to the computer network are all potential access points to the organisation's information and must, therefore, be rigorously controlled.

Environmental controls

The auditor must also be concerned with the risks of fire, flood, vandalism, sabotage and theft and the adequacy of insurance cover.

System issues

In conducting a review of a computerised system, the auditor must recognise that methods of processing and the nature of computing facilities will vary but, whatever the technology, the auditor is essentially concerned with the controls within the framework of a system's cycle; that is, input, processing and output. In addition, the auditor will be concerned to ensure that the system's design allows for an individual transaction to be traced through this cycle by means of the management or audit trail. The auditor will need, therefore, to focus upon four key areas: input, processing and output controls and an audit trail.

Input controls

The procedures adopted to control input to the system should, as far as is reasonably possible, ensure that it is genuine, complete, not previously processed, accurate and timely.

Processing controls

The processing controls within the computer system should ensure that the correct data and program files are used, that all data are processed, accounted for and written to the appropriate file, and that data conform to predetermined standards or fall within specified parameter values.

Output controls

The output controls should ensure that all expected output is produced, that it is complete, appears reasonable and is distributed on time and in such a way that confidentiality is maintained as necessary. Adequate controls should ensure that errors and exceptions are properly investigated and resubmissions of data made where appropriate.

Audit trail

A complete audit trail should be maintained which allows for both an item to be traced from input through to its final resting place, and a final result to be broken into its constituent parts.

The auditor's review of a system's controls might be applied to either a developing system or a live system. The overall audit objective applies in either case, though in the audit of a developing system the auditor is attempting to ascertain whether the controls to be incorporated within the system will allow adequate protection when the system becomes operational.

Legislation

The Data Protection Act 1984 imposed an obligation upon all users of computerised personal data to ensure that adequate security was provided. This legislative requirement can usefully be applied by audit to emphasise that there is an obligation upon users to give consideration to protecting computerised data and that a failure to do so which resulted in unauthorised disclosure of personal data would render the user to be personally liable.

The Computer Misuse Act made computer hacking an offence.

Computer assisted audit techniques

When auditing in a computerised environment, the auditor should consider using the computer as a direct aid to the audit. Data retrieval is the most widely used, most clearly understood and most easily obtainable of all the computer-assisted audit techniques (CAATs). It is most commonly used for extracting and manipulating data on magnetic files, for testing that data and for formatting reports for audit purposes. It can also be used to test the way programmed procedures and controls have operated on processed live data.

Audit use of software can assist all auditors in achieving their objectives. The long-term aim should be to put the whole of the audit section in a position to use the computer effectively and to allow the specialist auditor to operate as an adviser, giving technical support, developing audit techniques and dealing with those areas of computing which require a high level of technical skill.

Computer retrieval software is essentially an audit tool, used to test and verify the quality of data held on computer files and the adequacy and proper functioning of controls built into computer applications. Clearly, such tests are aimed at processing controls which form a part, albeit a significant part, of the audit of a live system. When viewed in this context, it will be appreciated that the use of computer retrieval software is only a beginning, though a most effective way of breaking into the other areas of computer audit. Through the use of retrieval software, the auditor will meet and discuss the contents of data files and computer applications with key computer personnel. Besides establishing channels of communications, this will develop the auditor's understanding of systems design and therefore improve confidence. Much of this knowledge acquired during the development of interrogation programs will have a direct bearing on the auditor's effectiveness in the other areas of auditing in a computerised environment.

CHAPTER 9
Contract audit

A contract is made whenever one party offers to supply something for a price and the other party accepts. It does not have to be in writing and so whenever an organisation buys anything it will be entering into a contract. There are clearly advantages in committing the terms of a contract into writing. An important function is to match expectations since the purchaser and supplier then both know what is to be supplied for what price and their respective responsibilities. It also provides a foundation for negotiation if the outcome of the contract does not proceed as expected. If significant problems occur, then both parties will (possibly without acknowledging this to each other) look at the contract terms to determine the respective strength of their negotiating positions. If the contract clearly defines what is to be supplied to what quality by what date, the purchaser can be more forceful in demanding a proper solution to any problem. It provides, too a means of protection if all goes wrong.

As well as the practical need for a clear contractual framework, there are two sets of rules which have to be followed: the Directives from the European Commission (EC) and the organisation's own Standing Orders. If these rules are not observed, there is a risk of legal challenge which could seriously delay the contract process and could result in a court order either suspending the contract process or awarding damages to a disappointed supplier. In summary, contractual negotiation is the most precise method available for evaluating the contents of a supplier's proposal and risks to the purchaser.

Public authorities spend vast sums of money each year under contracts. They range from large-scale capital procurements to smaller contracts for specific services – office cleaning, for example. In recent years there has been more focus on service contracts as more internal services are put forward for market testing under the Government's *Competing for Quality* programme, and a shift away in local authorities, for example, from large-scale capital developments. Nevertheless, the need to get the contract right is not diminished in any way and the auditor has a contribution to make in helping management to minimise difficulties which can occur if contracts are badly framed or poorly managed.

Understanding the EC rules

One of the EC objectives is to eliminate discrimination in the award of contracts on the basis of nationality, supplier or the origin of goods or services. The objectives are to be achieved by increasing competition within the single European Market by requiring 'contracting authorities' to let contracts over certain financial thresholds after the placing of advertisements and in accordance with prescribed procedures concerning content of specifications, invitation, receipt, opening and evaluation of tenders.

Contracting organisations are defined as bodies governed by 'public law', which includes public utilities, local authorities, health authorities and trusts, government departments, education, fire and police authorities. It should be noted that government departments and the health authorities are also required to comply with the General Agreement on Tariffs and Trade (GATT) regulations which impose further obligations on purchasing bodies.

The public procurement directives are based on three main objectives.

1. Community-wide advertising of contracts so that firms in all Member States have an opportunity to submit tenders.
2. The banning of national technical specifications liable to discriminate against potential foreign tenderers.
3. The application of objective criteria in tendering and award procedures to achieve a higher degree of transparency.

The directives which impact upon public procurement include the following:

- *The Works Directive (71/305/EEC as amended by 89/440/EEC)* This sets down rules for the award of contracts for construction or civil engineering works in the public sector where the contract value is equal to or above the specified limit. (From January 1992 the limit is 5 million European Currency Units (ECUs) which equates to £3.538m, net of VAT.)
- *The Supplies Directive (77/62/EEC as amended by 88/295/EEC)* This covers the purchase, lease, rental or hire of goods in the public sector where the intention is to let a contract or series of contracts whose value is equal to or above the specified limit. (From January 1992 the limit is 200,000 European Currency Units (ECUs) which equates to £141,431, net of VAT.)
- *The Compliance Directive (89/665/EEC)* This allows suppliers and contractors to bring proceedings in a national court of law if they are harmed by a breach of duty owed to them under the works or supplies directives.
- *The Services Directive (92/50/EEC, effective from July 1993)* This covers a range of professional and technical services where the contract value is above the threshold limit.

The role of internal audit

Internal audit should review procedures within their own organisation, to ensure that adherence to these directives is achieved with the minimum of disruption and additional cost. Audit should, therefore, take action as follows:

1. They should become acquainted with the EC directives themselves.
2. They should examine whether their organisation has appointed an officer with responsibility for assimilating and interpreting EC directives and offering guidance to appropriate heads of department. This is a key control in ensuring that the activities of the organisation in respect of EC matters are co-ordinated.
3. They should review appropriate systems, such as tendering procedures, to determine whether they comply with EC directives.

Internal auditors should adopt a systems-based approach when auditing contracts and, as with any such audit, this first requires the identification of control objectives and the appropriate key controls. Having reviewed compliance with the EC directives, the approach should be as follows:

- Assess and report on the adequacy of the organisation's standing orders relating to the contracts and associated financial regulations.
- Review and report on the extent to which procedures comply with the policies and procedural rules of the organisation.
- Review the adequacy of systems for controlling the operation of contracts from the initial planning stage to post-completion assessment.
- Review and report on the extent to which management information is prompt, adequate, accurate and designed for the needs of all the users in respect of the contract.
- Appraise the system for controlling and recording the utilisation of resources, including staff.
- Review the use of consultants and agency services provided by other organisations as part of the contract.
- Monitor the arrangements for the security of the organisation's assets and for recovering the cost of any rechargeable works.
- Prevent and detect opportunities for corruption, fraud, error and impropriety.
- Identify losses due to waste and inefficiency, and advise management how best to recover losses where appropriate.

CHAPTER 10
Fraud and corruption

It is more than likely that an auditor in the public sector will be required to investigate a fraud at some stage. A fraud investigation requires specialised knowledge and techniques, and needs to be handled with extreme care. Any mismanagement of a potential fraud could have far-reaching consequences. Very little has been published on the subject of fraud and corruption and there are only limited opportunities for auditors to gain experience and become proficient in this type of investigation. In fact, most experience is gained from an actual fraud investigation.

This chapter provides a review of the auditor's responsibility in fraud investigation, and includes attitudes towards fraud, some fraud statistics, types of fraud, the issues to be considered during a fraud investigation, including referral to the police, and a brief mention of the delicate subject of corruption. However, there is no set pattern to fraud investigation. Virtually every fraud investigation is different and it is not possible to devise a comprehensive set of rules which can be applied in all circumstances. The auditor must still apply judgement and intuition.

Auditor's responsibility for fraud

The APB guideline argues that it is management's responsibility to maintain the internal control system and to ensure that the organisation's resources are properly applied in the manner and on the activities intended and that this includes responsibility for the prevention and detection of fraud and other illegal acts. A related APB auditing guideline, *Fraud, Irregularities and Errors*, published in February 1990 states that 'the responsibility within an entity for the prevention of fraud, other irregularities and error rests with management.'

As an aid to management, the internal auditor must have regard to the possibility of such incidents and should seek to identify serious defects in internal control which might permit the occurrence of such an event. An internal auditor who discovers evidence of, or suspects, malpractice should report firm evidence, or reasonable suspicions, to the appropriate level of management. It is then management's responsibility to determine what further action to take.

While there may be a perception within an organisation that audit has a key role to play in relation to fraud, it is important that the role is defined so that the extent of audit involvement is clearly understood. In practice, audit may well have a responsibility to advise the organisation, investigate incidents and to call the police. There is a need, though, to balance the use of audit resources and here much depends upon the relations with the local police authority. It is not audit's task to take on the work of the police but it does need to liaise and the respective duties should be defined. A framework for audit involvement in fraud investigation and prosecution should be set down and reflected within the organisation's financial regulations.

Extent of fraud

Information on the extent of fraud within the public and private sectors is not readily available. The absence of any statutory obligation upon organisations to disclose fraud hampers any attempt to provide a reliable estimate of the extent of the abuse but it is sufficient perhaps to recognise that those activities which are reported are only the tip of the proverbial iceberg. Incidents of fraud and corruption fall into three categories:

1. Those which are known and recorded publicly.
2. Those which are known only within organisations and which will not be brought into the public arena.
3. Those which are, as yet, undiscovered.

In 1992, the Home Office reported some 168,000 notifiable offences with around 94,000 being cleared up, but the full extent of fraud losses in the UK business community is not known although many estimates are available: the CBI, for example, estimated in 1990 that some £3,000 million was lost annually. Within the public sector, some of the external audit bodies publish information on the extent of fraud within their respective areas of responsibility but there is no obligation upon them to do so and a full picture of public sector fraud does not exist.

Two particular bodies – the Audit Commission and the National Audit Office – provide information on the type and range of frauds known to have occurred in the local government and National Health Service, and in central government bodies. Neither organisation claims to publish a definitive list of frauds but the information is helpful in illustrating the range and scale of current frauds.

Local government

In an analysis of frauds reported by the Commission for the nine years ended March 1993, around £16 million worth of frauds was recorded. Income frauds totalled around £4 million, cash frauds around £555,000, stores and goods frauds around £556,000 and the remaining £11 million related to expenditure frauds.

The largest number of income frauds involved fines and fees and car parking takings. Most expenditure frauds related to creditor payments and to the payment of benefits.

An analysis of perpetrators of fraud found that outsiders committed most frauds and that the most usual method was the submission of false claims, the retention of cash and the misappropriation of cheques.

National Health Service

Some 15 frauds in the National Health Service were reported for 1992/93 and they totalled a little over £270,000. Most expenditure frauds occurred in pay and allowances systems; and retention of income from telephone calls was the cause of most income frauds.

Central government

Information on frauds occurring in central government departments is published in individual reports by the Comptroller and Auditor General. Examples of cases include TV licence evasion (£130 million reported in August 1989), Vehicle Excise Duty evasion (£105 million reported in 1990/91) and Inland Revenue frauds (£792,000 in 1990/91). Contractors to the Property Services Agency (PSA) defrauded it of £1.68 million on supply and works contracts in 1990, and stores frauds in the Ministry of Defence totalled £450,000 in 1989.

Computer frauds

Most financial systems are now computerised and where frauds occur they frequently involve the computer process but while claims are frequently made as to the extent of losses caused by computer fraud and abuse, they are rarely if ever substantiated. The Audit Commission conducts triennial surveys of computer fraud and abuse throughout the public and private sectors with the aim of providing an indication of the nature of the risks which organisations face when relying upon technology to support their business activities.

Over 1,500 organisations responded to the 1990 Survey and 180 incidents were reported with a total direct loss of over £1 million. Frauds accounted for 73 of the cases and there were 27 instances of theft, 26 hacking incidents and 54 virus attacks. In comparison with the results of previous surveys, frauds have continued to rise whilst other types of incidents have varied in frequency. Around 44% of all of these incidents occurred in public sector organisations.

Traditionally, the unauthorised alteration of data prior to inputting into the computer together with the alteration of computerised data accounted for the largest single number of fraud incidents. The destruction or suppression or misappropriation of output and the alteration or misuse of programs accounted in the past for very few instances of fraud. Output and program frauds now represent a larger share of the overall number of fraud cases although input frauds still dominate overall.

When compared with earlier surveys, it is evident that there has been an increase in the number of expenditure, as opposed to income system frauds. More frauds are being perpetrated through submission of unauthorised invoices and claims or the alteration of computerised payment data. The increasing dependence upon online systems to cope with claimants' payment systems makes such applications prone to fraud if safeguards are not built into the clerical and computerised processes. The absence of an adequate division of responsibilities with the onus being placed upon a single terminal operator to deal directly and wholly with claimants may at first sight seem efficient and cost-effective. The costs of that arrangement must be weighed against the risks of such an individual being able to create fictitious claimants' records and make payments through an automated payments system direct to a bank account.

One of the disturbing findings of the survey was that internal control accounted for only 23% of the total number of detections. Audit discovered around 14% of the cases and, while audit's primary role is not to detect frauds, it does have a responsibility to make management aware of the need for adequate controls and the consequences of their not being in place. With internal control having such a marked lack of effect, audit may well need to re-assess the effectiveness of its role in highlighting risks and helping to install mechanisms which inhibit fraud. Most frauds were made possible by the absence of basic controls and safeguards and often the lack of the 'textbook' control provided the opportunity for the fraud to be perpetrated. This is a message which seems relevant to all cases of fraud.

Attitudes to fraud

Once it has been established that a fraud has been committed, an important consideration in any fraud investigation is to decide on the line to be taken. There is one line which says 'the least said, the better' and which seeks to avoid any risk of the sort of adverse publicity which court proceedings are likely to attract. A more forthright attitude for management to adopt, particularly in the public sector, is to accept that it is the duty of any citizen to report criminal activities to the police and to expect the due processes of law to follow. In fact, the Criminal Law Act 1967 makes it a general offence to act with the intention of impeding the apprehension or prosecution of offenders for arrestable offences without lawful authority or reasonable excuse.

However, the circumstances of a fraud must be taken into account in considering whether to refer the matter to the police. A public authority may be justified in not referring a case where the amount stolen is small, or where there are other mitigating factors, such as illness of the perpetrator. As a general rule, however, most frauds in the public sector should be referred to the police who should decide on prosecution. Furthermore, it should be noted that it is often a condition of fidelity guarantee insurance policies that the police are informed of frauds.

Types of fraud

Basic frauds

Basic frauds arise primarily because of a breakdown in systems. Typical basic frauds are listed and discussed below.

Income

The retention or the misappropriation of cash is the simplest and most usual type of fraud. Examples include the misappropriation of collections, rents and car parking fees. Income frauds can, as a general rule, be detected by the careful monitoring of the regularity of banking, though it is not audit's responsibility to monitor the regularity of banking on a routine basis: this should be the role of a central income section, which could usefully employ a computerised system to monitor actual receipts from accountable officers, units, establishments, etc., against a predetermined norm on a weekly basis and to highlight significant deviations.

Expenditure

This involves fictitious payments, purchases and petty cash payments. Frauds occurring in this area arise because of weaknesses in internal control. Examples of such frauds include the falsification of pension refund vouchers, fictitious vouchers for the payment of expenses and submission of false invoices. To explore some of the opportunities for fraud it is worth asking the following questions:

- What controls are employed to see that the correct quality and quantity of goods are supplied?
- What checks are made regarding possible collusion between contractors to fix prices?

- Who delivers the items contained within the contract? Is it the firm that was awarded the contract?
- Are company searches on firms on approved tender lists carried out to establish whether any links exist between the various firms or even whether the organisation's employees are recorded as directors?
- What controls are in evidence over price increases in, for example, energy contracts?

False wages/salary claims

These are a common occurrence in the public sector, but many examples of frauds which have arisen in this area have occurred because of a violation of the principles of internal check. Examples include overclaimed overtime, falsification of time sheets through inflation of hours worked, and fictitious claims.

Theft of equipment and stores

Inventories may be out of date, or even non-existent, and frequently security arrangements are related only to break-ins and may not cover the possibility of theft by employees. In such circumstances, employees may be able to steal equipment and stores almost with impunity, whilst the petty cash is well protected. Typical frauds of this nature are theft of car spares from transport depots, theft of materials (such as paint, wood, fittings, etc.) from direct labour units, and theft of valuable exhibits from museums.

Falsification of travelling and subsistence claims

These are fairly common occurrences for internal audit to investigate. Once again, any frauds occurring generally arise from a breakdown in internal control, with the person responsible for certifying the claim not checking it properly.

Corruption

It is absolutely vital that the auditor is aware of the possibility of corruption when undertaking audit investigations. Although fairly obvious, it is important that the auditor takes the following items of evidence into consideration where corruption is concerned:

1. Rumours of a manager living beyond his means.
2. Tales of high living.
3. Frequent visits to the office by certain contractors to see a manager.
4. Car registration details.

5. Indication (from an examination of travelling claims) of frequent visits to a contractor by a manager.

Practical aspects of fraud investigation

It has already been stressed that there is no set pattern to a fraud investigation. The auditor must apply judgement and intuition and respond to 'tip-offs' and rumours – there is a tendency for personnel to inform the auditor and then abrogate responsibility. The auditor cannot afford to ignore such information, however scant; to do so could cause serious problems, particularly if fraud were detected sometime later. However, it must be borne in mind that anonymous statements are sometimes made for malicious reasons. Time, patience and planning are particularly important in any fraud investigations. Auditors should not rush into an investigation since one of the great dangers is in alerting the guilty party.

The auditor's task is to investigate and establish fraud and ascertain its extent. This work can, without doubt, be undertaken more efficiently if the procedures to be followed are defined in advance. Unless investigations are conducted carefully and in a disciplined way an oversight or transgression may occur which, at a later point of the enquiry, could at least be embarrassing or at worst prevent the successful prosecution or dismissal of a defaulter.

These considerations apply to the conduct of a fraud investigation no matter how the irregularity comes to the auditor's notice. If it is brought to light by a third party, however, the auditor's first step must be to check the alleged facts. This must be done as soon as possible, but not before all the relevant information relating to the offender and his/her responsibilities has been assembled. The procedure is similar to the preparation for an audit visit and, in fact, such investigations are frequently carried out in the guise of a normal audit. It is desirable that two auditors should be present at all stages of a fraud investigation.

Where the auditor is satisfied that there are grounds for thinking that a fraud has been committed he/she should do the following:

1. Carefully check the facts again.
2. Restrict questioning to establishing that the suspicion appears to be well founded.
3. Retain all records which may be involved, bearing in mind when handling documents that finger-printing or other forensic examination may take place later.
4. Establish all the areas of activity of the person under suspicion in order to gauge the potential size of the fraud.
5. If necessary, telephone the audit manager to inform him/her of the facts and to seek guidance. Depending upon the circumstances, this call should be made from an outside telephone.

At this early stage it is important to establish a file for the investigation. All material should be assembled chronologically and a dated index of progress should be maintained, together with detailed notes of all relevant interviews, meetings and decisions taken. In maintaining this file, auditors should be aware that it may become evidence in a court of law or at an industrial tribunal considering an appeal against unfair dismissal.

The objectives of the investigation will be as follows:

1. To collect sufficient evidence to prove the offence and to identify the defaulter.
2. To have the employee suspended while a full investigation is completed.
3. To provide evidence for disciplinary or legal action.

It is not possible to detail the work needed to achieve the foregoing – the circumstances of each case will dictate what is needed. However, the auditor must be particularly alert to ascertain the full extent of the fraud and any related frauds; he/she must be painstaking and particularly careful bearing in mind that any action or omissions may subsequently be very closely examined in a court of law or an industrial tribunal.

Relationship with police

At this stage, it is worth stressing that it is extremely useful for the audit manager to build up an effective liaison between the police and the audit sections. This relationship is vital for both parties and there must be close co-operation and a great deal of trust. If such a link is established, the expertise of the police, on an informal basis, is available to the auditor in planning the course of an investigation into a potential fraud. It is possible to discuss with the police the facts which are available, without having to ask them to investigate the matter. In addition, it may be that the police can produce some information, or at least suggest you acquire certain items to assist you. Certainly, the value of the advice of the police should not be underrated. It is also possible to overcome the problem of deciding when a case should be referred to the police and, in particular, in deciding whether audit should interview the suspect first (or even at all) before handing the case over to the police.

The question of how soon the police should be informed officially is always a difficult one. In theory, the police should be informed as soon as there are reasonable grounds for suspecting that a criminal offence has been committed. In practice, it is a matter for local judgement, based on the facts of each individual case, but the informal relationship mentioned earlier can be of great assistance. However, for general guidance, the following are suggested times to inform the police:

1. *Immediately*: when there are suspicions of corrupt practice.

2. *Before interviews take place*: when there is some evidence of systematic theft but it needs to be confirmed by witnessed observation if the case is to be made for criminal prosecution.
3. *As soon as fraud has been established*: when the defaulter cannot be identified from the accounting records (e.g. fraudulent encashment of a cheque).
4. *Probably after the first interview*: when the records indicate fraud by a particular person. It is useful to have the interview to confirm the evidence of the records and to suspend the offender while further enquiries are made.

In deciding when to involve the police, it must be remembered that the auditor, however much this seems attractive, should not take over the role of the police to 'obtain' a confession. The police are skilled interrogators and should be brought in as soon as circumstances warrant it.

It is appropriate to mention briefly the area of surveillance. As a general rule this should be done by the police but, from time to time, internal audit needs to undertake some observation before the police are involved, either formally or informally. Where the surveillance is undertaken in order to provide evidence, it is vital that the original notes of the observations are recorded, signed and dated immediately by the person making them. Records should be kept of all the details noted or checks undertaken. It is also useful to warn the police before undertaking surveillance work to avoid the embarrassment of auditors being reported for suspicious activity! Finally, a man and woman from internal audit look far less obvious than two men when surveillance is being undertaken.

Planning and conducting the interview

The Police and Criminal Evidence Act 1984 (PACE) provided guidance on how investigations should be conducted and the auditor should be familiar with this legislation. CIPFA's publication *The investigation of fraud in the public sector* also provides valuable detailed guidance on the subject.

When it has been decided, or circumstances dictate, that the auditor will have to interview the suspect during the course of a fraud investigation, it is useful to undertake some careful planning for the interview. Basically there are three stages – before the interview, during the interview and after it – and each is considered in turn.

Before conducting an interview, the auditor should consider the following points:

1. On what aspects is information required? One approach is to prepare the questions in advance of the interview. This has much to commend it since it presents a structured plan of action. However, if this is done, the auditor must realise that supplementary questions may be needed during the

interview. If the questions are not written in advance, then at least a written checklist is required.

2. The time and place for the interview must be fixed, bearing in mind the need to avoid any interruptions. If there is a break in a formal interview, the interviewee might take advantage of this to fabricate an explanation, destroy evidence or even 'tip off' a colleague. Formal interviews tend to be quite lengthy, and clearly it is important to avoid the discussion going beyond normal working hours; otherwise the interviewee might justifiably refuse to continue. Consequently, a late start should be avoided; and, as a general rule, the best time and place to hold a formal interview is either early in the morning or immediately after lunch at a location away from the interviewee's normal place of work.

3. Who will be present? It is important to have as few people as possible present whilst, at the same time, ensuring that all interested parties are represented. Two auditors should be present, mainly to ensure that a reliable witness to the proceedings is available. As a general rule, one auditor should ask the questions and the second should make such notes as are necessary. It may be useful to have present a manager from the interviewee's department who has the power to suspend the employee if necessary.

4. The interviewee should be advised of the time and place of the interview and given a very brief indication about the matter to be discussed. However, the auditor should not be too specific about this for the obvious reason of not helping the suspect to devise a defence or to destroy evidence.

5. The interviewee may ask to be accompanied by a companion who may be a representative from the union. This practice seems to be increasing; however, at this stage, the advice would be for the auditor to resist it since he/she is only seeking explanations: it is not a formal disciplinary hearing. However, if the request is conceded, then it must be under the strict understanding that the companion is present as an observer only.

The following are some useful hints on *procedure at the actual interview*:

1. As a general rule, one auditor should ask the questions and the second should make notes.

2. It is vital that nothing is done at the interview which could be construed as duress by the interviewee. No statement by an accused person is admissible in evidence against him/her unless it can be shown by the prosecution to have been made voluntarily. Consequently, the auditor must not make any threats or promises, actual or implied, in order to obtain a statement.

3. The auditor should make it clear to the interviewee that the auditor is conducting the interview. This may be difficult if a senior person is present from the employee's department, but it is a point worth resolving in advance.

4. It may be useful to begin the interview by asking the interviewee to outline his/her understanding of his/her duties and responsibilities in connection with the matter under review. It needs to be established whether the duties were explained to the interviewee and, if so, by whom. Any such statement should be carefully noted and may provide a useful base for subsequent disciplinary action.

5. Great skill and care must be exercised in framing questions. Making statements should be avoided since the objective is to concentrate on asking questions in order to obtain answers. Any evasive answers must be followed up by supplementary questions. It is important that the auditor covers all the ground to be discussed at the interview without the need for adjournments which could be used to advantage by the interviewee.

6. If two or more people are implicated in a potential fraud, then it is imperative that the auditors prevent them from making contact between individual interviews and creating alibis.

7. If, during the course of an interview, the auditor forms the opinion that he/she has reasonable grounds for believing the interviewee has committed an offence, or if the interviewee admits to an offence, then that is the time to conclude the interview. The suspect should not be pressed to make a statement because the police will be able to do that more effectively and, if they are to consider prosecution, they will prefer to take the statement themselves.

8. The suspect might insist on making a statement, however, and in this case he/she should be allowed to do so. It is imperative that the auditor is familiar with the application of the Judges' Rules so that the statement obtained is admissible as evidence in court. (It should be noted that the Judges' Rules do not apply in Scotland, but they form a useful guideline for Scottish auditors.) Under such circumstances, the auditor must apply the caution in the following terms:

> *You are not obliged to say anything unless you wish to do so, but what you say may be put into writing and given in evidence.*

The Rules continue as follows:

> *When, after being cautioned, a person is being questioned, or elects to make a statement, a record shall be kept of the time and place at which any such questioning or statement began and ended and of the persons present.*

The statement must be given on a voluntary basis and not as a result of any real or implied threat or promise. It is suggested that the statement begins with a paragraph such as the following:

> *I make this statement of my own free will. I have been told that I need not say anything unless I wish to do so and that whatever I say may be given in evidence.*

When the statement has been completed, it should be signed and the signature must be witnessed.

9. Where no written statement is taken from a suspect during an interview, the auditor's notes have the potential of becoming important evidence if criminal charges result. The auditor should keep this in mind when taking and writing up the notes which should be agreed, signed and dated by both auditors as soon as possible after the interview.

10. At the conclusion of the interview, the auditor must make sure that he/she obtains possession of any original documents which may be required as evidence. Finally, he/she must be aware that the security of audit working papers is absolutely crucial. This may sound obvious, but a case was reported of a fraud investigation where the audit working papers and notes were left out overnight. They disappeared. So did the fraud investigation!

It is quite easy for an auditor to forget some of the actions that are required to be taken *after an interview* which has produced reasonable grounds for believing that fraud has occurred. Some vital actions are as follows:

1. *Suspension* This should be the final decision at the conclusion of the interview; normally an employee will be suspended on full pay, but it might be possible to arrange a suspension without pay. Of course, it is not the role of the auditor to suspend but that of line management. If the employee admits to a fraud, then instant dismissal may be a possibility (see below).

2. *Leaving the building* The offender should be accompanied from the interview back to his/her place of work to collect, under supervision, any personal belongings. It is vital that records which might assist the subsequent investigation are not removed or destroyed. The offender should be escorted off the premises and allowed no further access without the approval of the auditor in charge of the investigation.

3. *Informing the police* The police need to be informed of the outcome of the interview as a matter of urgency.

4. *Dismissal* In order to minimise the increasing loss to the organisation represented by suspension pay, dismissal should be considered as soon as there are adequate grounds. This can be done before any criminal prosecution is made and, possibly, in large or complex frauds, even before the full extent of the loss is known.

5. *Insurance* It is normally a requirement that the insurers are informed of the possibility of a claim.

6. *Recovery of loss* It may be possible, in certain circumstances, to recover the amount of any loss from the appropriate pension fund. In local government, the external auditors have powers to declare amounts due where losses have occurred through wilful misconduct. In criminal cases, it is possible to ask the court to make an order for restitution.

7. *Informing the external auditor* Internal audit should make the external auditor aware of the fraud immediately (and vice versa). Whichever auditor is involved should inform his/her counterpart in order to prevent duplication of effort, to exchange relevant information and to prevent any difficulties which could arise if the other auditor did, possibly coincidentally, have any reason to become involved with the suspect concerning the fraud or some other unrelated matter.

7. *System review* A full investigation of the circumstances surrounding the fraudulent occurrences must be undertaken, the system must be evaluated and proposals for strengthening it (if a system weakness is found) must be agreed upon and implemented.

9. *Recording of irregularities* As part of the management of the audit section, a record file of irregularities should be maintained.

Conclusion

'Honesty is frequent and dull; fraud is rare but stimulating,' some people say. Fraud investigation is perhaps the most exciting and exacting aspect of audit work and any investigation must, therefore, be conducted with the utmost tact and with a determination to establish the facts and bring the matter to a conclusion as soon as possible. All frauds are different and the need for flexibility in approach during an investigation is of paramount importance, with a high degree of urgency required of the investigating officer.

CHAPTER 11
The internal auditor and value for money

Value for money is an extremely wide-ranging topic, with implications for every activity undertaken by an organisation. It is almost impossible to produce a definition of value for money that will satisfy everyone's interpretation. Such is the nature of the concept that definitions range from 'the cheapest unit cost' at one end of the scale to 'the best possible quality' at the other. Value for money must encompass a balance between inputs and the service provided. Implicit in this is a pre-specification of the level of service that is required in terms of quality and quantity. Value for money represents achieving that level of service at the most economical cost. It follows, therefore, that the lowest unit cost does not always represent the best value for money and, indeed, the cheapest solution is not necessarily the best.

Responsibility for value for money

Everyone associated with an organisation has some responsibility for value for money but the prime responsibility lies with management. The auditor's role must be to assist management in its responsibility, and it must be stressed that the achievement of value for money relies heavily upon the right attitude being present at all levels in the organisation. Management's aim should be to encourage an environment which is conducive to optimum value for money. Unless the people working for an organisation genuinely want to achieve value for money, then all the systems and procedures in the world will be to no avail.

Value for money audit

Value for money (VFM) audit is, broadly speaking, a function provided by the auditor with the aim of identifying and recommending to the management of an audited body, ways in which the organisation's return for the resources which it employs in pursuing its objectives may be maximised. It is a function practised by both internal and external auditors, and the pioneering work by the latter in the 1970s has helped focus and sustain the significance of the subject.

The responsibilities of internal audit in relation to VFM are described in the APB guideline as assisting 'management in the pursuit of value for money. It is achieved through economic, efficient and effective use of resources.' External auditors, generally, are exhorted to review VFM through the APB guideline *Reports to Management* where it says, 'The auditor may also wish to include in the report comments on potential economies, improvements in efficiency, or other constructive advice which might be of assistance to the client organisation.' More specific obligations upon external audit are embodied in statute. The Audit Commission, Accounts Commission and National Audit Office are all required to review VFM as part of their normal audits. More information on their respective responsibilities is contained in subsequent chapters in this book.

Structural organisation

Some audit managers, particularly in the field of internal audit, set up separate teams to deal with value for money. These units have been given such names as 'Cost Effectiveness Unit', 'Value Review Team' and 'Management Audit Group'. The objective has been to set aside staff with a particular aptitude for value for money work and, in so doing, to create a team which will develop experience and expertise in this field, unencumbered with the more routine aspects of audit work. This approach has worked well in many organisations but, set against its undoubted benefits, there must be a number of disadvantages:

- The value for money specialist will not have the detailed knowledge that the 'service auditor' has and thus it may take longer to carry out the necessary research work.
- Valuable departmental contacts built up by the 'service auditor' may not be available to the value for money team.
- The creation of what may be regarded as an elite value for money team may have a demoralising effect on the audit staff who are not selected to be members of that team.

Increasingly within many audit sections, value for money work is seen as an integral part of the audit task, and a specific allocation of time is not thought to be appropriate. Auditors are required to have regard to value for money issues whilst conducting systems-based and transaction-based audits. In other organisations, though, a separate allocation is made for value for money studies and individual exercises are planned. In this way, the audit manager can be sure that specific attention is directed to the need to achieve value for money and resources can be concentrated upon areas of known poor performance which, incidentally, may well have been identified during systems-based and transaction-based audits.

The three Es

It may be helpful at this stage to discuss what have become recognised as the three pillars of VFM – the three Es:

1. *Economy*.
2. *Efficiency*.
3. *Effectiveness*.

Economy is the relationship between the market and inputs. In other words, it is the practice of buying goods and services of the desired quality at the best possible price. An activity would not be economic, for example, if there was overstaffing or failure to purchase materials of the right quality at the lowest available price.

Efficiency is the relationship between inputs and outputs: it is the efficient use of the minimum goods and services required to achieve the desired maximum level of outputs.

Effectiveness is the relationship between outputs and objectives. In other words, it is a measure of the extent to which the organisation's outputs, policies and procedures achieve its stated objectives.

The auditor's role with regard to the first two Es is rarely challenged. Who would argue that the auditor has a duty to ensure that resources are acquired as economically as possible and that those resources are then used in the most efficient manner? However, it is when the auditor becomes involved in effectiveness that problems may be encountered. When the auditor begins to question how effective an organisation's policies are in achieving its defined objectives there may well be resistance; yet, if the auditor is to meet the objectives defined in the APB guideline, the effectiveness of policies must be evaluated.

Logically, the auditor's approach to value for money should be to determine what the objectives of the organisation are – not the easiest of tasks with many public sector bodies. The auditor must then ascertain the policies which have been adopted to achieve those objectives. The auditor's task then involves an appraisal of the effectiveness of those policies and the economy and efficiency with which they are carried out.

Planning a VFM audit

There is no set procedure for planning or undertaking a VFM audit. Identifying fruitful areas for review is clearly important and the auditor should have regard to the overall scale, policy and objectives of the organisation to help identify those areas where close attention to VFM issues will be most fruitful. It has already been stated that the prime responsibility for ensuring that value for money is achieved rests firmly with management. The auditor's role is to review the effectiveness of the systems which management use to monitor value for money and to ensure that positive and effective action is taken whenever poor value for money is identified. Up to this point the role is common to both the internal auditor and the external counterpart. However, the internal auditor is much more likely to develop a role beyond this stage. Aside from the 'systems' approach to value for money, auditors will often become involved in value for money projects. Such projects can conveniently be broken down into five distinct stages, as follows:

1. The identification of an area where, prima facie, there is evidence of poor value for money.
2. The detailed investigation of that area to establish the facts.
3. The development of proposals to remedy the situation.
4. The implementation of those proposals.
5. Monitoring the success of the remedy.

Whilst it could never be argued that the first stage is the sole responsibility of the auditor (indeed, everyone has a part to play in this), no one would dispute that the auditor has a function to fulfil in this respect and, in many ways, is ideally suited to carry out that function. So far as the second stage is concerned arrangements will vary, but there is no doubt that the detailed knowledge built up by the auditor, together with investigative skills, will facilitate assistance considerably at this stage. The auditor needs to exercise care in being involved in the third stage, so as not to jeopardise future independence. Where management's resources are so restricted or its investigative skills so limited as to render impossible the development of suitable solutions to the problems, then the auditor may find it necessary and helpful to assist. However, the auditor should ensure that management agrees and takes ownership of the proposals. The fourth stage is purely a matter for management and the auditor should not become involved. As far as monitoring is concerned, the responsibility must, again, lie largely with management, but there is no doubt that the auditor has a duty to ensure that management carries out this task, and perhaps one effective way of doing this is to monitor the success of the remedy personally.

Value review systems

Apart from the more common management accounting and costing systems, many additional procedures exist to assist management, and thus to assist the auditor to identify poor value for money. In a general publication of this nature, it is not appropriate to discuss these in depth; indeed, each one could merit a publication of its own. However, it will be helpful to identify some systems and to discuss briefly the extent to which they may be of use to the auditor. The more common systems are as follows:

- *Comparative studies and statistics* These must provide one of the most useful means of concentrating scarce investigatory resources into potentially lucrative areas. The auditor needs to remember that comparative statistics take no account of variations in sources of information, differing levels of service or of environmental factors which will, in many cases, undoubtedly account for differing costs. Such statistics should be treated, however, as a useful means of focusing audit attention on areas which may prove to be beneficial. CIPFA's Statistical Information Service and the Audit Commission's local government and NHS profiles all provide useful sources of data, for example. The use of comparative statistics need not be restricted to comparisons between organisations. Comparisons between similar units within an organisation, or from year to year in the same unit, are equally useful. Comparative studies are a natural development from comparative statistics. Where unit costs are found to differ considerably, it becomes necessary to study the differences in depth and to identify the causes. It is only in this way that a meaningful conclusion can be reached.

  The published national studies of the Audit Commission provide valuable comparative reviews of various local government and NHS services. The practice of the Commission's external auditors proceeding to conduct audit reviews at subsequent audits helps ensure greater focus upon the subjects and provides useful material for local management and auditors to conduct their own VFM reviews.

  The Citizens Charter initiative generally and the publication of performance indicators for local government services, in particular, has provided additional impetus to the drive for VFM by providing the individual with material on which to question the economy, efficiency and effectiveness of services provided to the public. The auditor will need to recognise the opportunity to review the procedures for collecting and calculating the various indicators to be published and to provide management with an independent view on their accuracy and completeness. They will also provide valuable comparative data on which to base further audit reviews.
- *Budgets and budgetary control* It is often argued that as they impose a cash constraint, budgets and budgetary control, play a major part in the development of value for money. Conversely, it can be argued with equal

conviction that incremental budgeting, combined with the annual year-end 'binge' to spend up to the target and thus protect next year's allocation, has precisely the opposite effect. One of the most useful exercises which an auditor can undertake is to 'audit the estimates' – in other words, to examine the system by which the estimates are compiled and to 'zero the base' on selected budget heads and rebuild the budget on a 'needs' rather than an 'incremental' basis.

- *Performance review committees* Increasingly organisations have established such groups to help identify the achievement of targets and to ensure that sufficient attention is being directed towards VFM issues. In a climate where economy, efficiency and effectiveness are key concerns, such committees assume more significance and it is important that the auditor's role in the process is established.
- *Selected invoices* Some organisations operate a system whereby a limited number of invoices are selected, at random or otherwise, and are subjected to detailed scrutiny, often by the auditor. Elected members are often involved in this process, which has the benefit of creating an environment where any invoice has the potential of coming under the microscope. In organisations that operate a process such as this, the certification of invoices ceases to be the automatic, robot-like process which it can sometimes become.

CHAPTER 12

Measuring the performance of audit

All public sector auditors, be they internal or external, are concerned with the effectiveness of the organisations they audit, but auditors themselves are not immune from an assessment of their performance which is rightly subject to scrutiny by others. There are continued and increasing pressures on available resources within the public sector and this scrutiny encourages audit managers to find ways of monitoring the use of their staff resources.

The APB guideline states that the audit manager should establish arrangements to evaluate the performance of the internal audit department and that an annual report may also be prepared for management on the activities of internal audit and in which an assessment is given of how effectively the objectives of the function have been met.

Audit, like other services, needs to be able to apply some measurement criteria to its performance to satisfy itself and its clients that it is providing an efficient, effective and economic service. It should also be recognised that not all public sector bodies are required to provide an internal audit service and so there is added pressure in such organisations for audit to be able to demonstrate its worth.

Performance indicators

Performance indicators help in achieving and demonstrating audit's worth but the use of such indicators is not without problems. Simple measures of time input to an audit are easily made but it is more difficult to comment on whether such time has been spent effectively. This is of interest not only to internal audit managers but also to their respective line managers, to their clients and to external auditors. There is a large number of potential indicators available but, as with any activity, it is important that they are analysed and applied sensibly.

Performance indicators should not be seen as ends in themselves. They are action tools for management who should apply them to decide how best to assess the success of audit. No one performance indicator provides a comprehensive view of audit's performance. Organisations should, therefore, compile a basket of indicators to provide an overall view of audit.

The warning or limitation which must go with any such indicators is that interpretation must be undertaken carefully and a broad, balanced view taken. Undue emphasis or reliance placed upon any single indicator or group of indicators will inevitably lead to a distorted view. Performance indicators cannot be used in isolation as reliable measures of performance, since other factors may also have to be taken into account. They can, however, help to highlight areas which appear to merit closer examination. For this reason, any review of indicators should be taken in conjunction with a general review of activities against standards which have been established, taking into account the relevant guidance from the Auditing Practices Board and from CIPFA.

Performance indicators should not be confused with normal management processes and controls even though certain indicators may appear to be similar in nature to key controls. It is important to recognise the distinction between the management controls, which form an integral part of a system, and the indicators, which seek to measure the economy, efficiency and effectiveness with which the objectives of that system are being met.

Much of the emphasis in written material on the subject has been on the measurement of *economy* and *efficiency*, concentrating on the assessment of inputs. *Economy* and *efficiency* indicators may include the following:

- Time spent on individual audits in comparison with planned time.
- Time spent on total audits in comparison with planned time.
- Percentage of planned audits completed in comparison with percentage of planned time used.
- Target dates for various stages of audits.
- Target period for issue of audit reports.

Rather less consideration has been given to *effectiveness*, whereby an attempt is made to measure outputs. This requires a wider perspective, and, as it is generally accepted that outputs are more difficult to measure, it is not surprising that less attention has been directed towards this area of audit's performance. It is important to be certain that not only goals are being achieved but also that they are worth achieving. *Effectiveness* indicators may include the following:

- Extent of critical expenditure and income systems reviewed and tested.
- Extent of audit cover plan achieved.
- Cost savings or increased opportunities identified by audit.
- Extent of audit recommendations accepted and implemented.
- Client satisfaction survey results.

• Occasions on which internal audit was consulted on system changes.

> Whether or not audit is able to perform the full range of audit functions effectively and efficiently largely depends upon management attitude and support which is itself influenced by status and independence. The real sign of independence is that auditors are not impeded in their efforts to examine any area within the organisation whereas status often determines the significance attached to audit findings by management.

This extract from CIPFA's occasional paper 'An approach to the measurement of the performance of internal audit', published in 1981, is still valid. Nevertheless, the responsibility for delivering an effective and efficient audit service also lies with audit management, and the present competitive climate should encourage audit to recognise that it must convince senior management that it is worth supporting.

Different individuals are interested in the performance of internal audit:

1. *Audit committees* (where appointed), who will wish to use audit to monitor the economy, efficiency and effectiveness of the organisation as well as its financial well-being.
2. *Management*, on whose behalf internal audit is expected to measure, evaluate and report upon the effectiveness of internal controls.
3. *The chief internal auditor*, who will want the audit section to have impact.
4. *External audit*, who need to place reliance on the work of internal audit.

To assess the effectiveness of internal audit, four fundamental questions should be considered:

1. Has internal audit established goals which have been agreed with their clients?
2. Will the achievement of these goals contribute to corporate objectives and effective internal control?
3. Is the work planned and resourced in such a way as to make achievement a realistic possibility?
4. Does internal audit achieve its defined goals?

The assessment of these points should provide a means of assessing audit's effectiveness through a review of internal audit's goals, inputs, processes and outputs.

The first question presents the least difficulty since well-established goals normally cannot exist without some form of tangible evidence. They should have been committed to writing and be available for all to see so that there is no misunderstanding of audit's role and objectives. Such evidence should usually be found in internal audit's business plan and terms of reference. Clearly, if management has failed to determine and document the role and objectives of internal audit it has little or no chance of monitoring its effectiveness.

Assuming internal audit's goals have been defined, then the second question may be answered by judging them against professional standards. The APB's internal audit guideline provides the good practice which should be adopted by internal auditors who are members of CCAB bodies and who work in public and private sector organisations. If audit's goals do meet with APB guidance then it is reasonable to conclude that its achievement would contribute to effective internal control.

Resources and working practices are reviewed as a means of measuring performance, and factors such as staffing, training, planning and reporting are considered. To answer the third question, therefore, a reviewer will need to consider such aspects as whether internal audit adopts a systems-based approach and whether its annual programme is of adequate scope and takes account of high risk areas (e.g. those involving cash handling), or changes in the organisation's main financial systems. It should be recognised, though, that high risk does not necessarily equate only with financial systems. Other systems may be more critical to the organisation's success.

Such an approach, however, will not provide the answer to the final effectiveness question – whether goals have been achieved. It will say only whether goals are *likely* to be achieved.

The APB guidelines represent an essential element in the establishment of high professional standards of internal audit practice amongst all internal auditors. If an internal audit section does not perform in accordance with these guidelines it is unlikely to be effective; but conforming is no absolute guarantee of effective output.

Output measurement

Those wishing to evaluate audit output should, therefore, exercise considerable care. The mere completion of an audit programme is no guarantee of effectiveness. On the other hand, it is too crude to measure effectiveness only in terms of discoveries of frauds, systems weaknesses and opportunities for savings – it is possible that there may be nothing to discover in the particular function subject to audit. Furthermore, the presence of an effective audit section has a deterrent effect which cannot be quantified.

There is, however, a small range of output measures which can be applied. At the outset a reviewer should establish if internal audit can account for itself by providing formal audit reports and an annual report, possibly direct to an audit committee. An initial impression of its effectiveness can be gained by considering the quality of findings and recommendations. This may be reinforced by establishing the number of frauds, system weaknesses and value for money opportunities which are discovered by other means or agencies, such as external audit, management, or members of the public.

Reviewing the action taken as a result of internal audit's work is probably the most powerful way of measuring its effectiveness. This process is made immeasurably easier where audit reports incorporate detailed action plans. The crucial question must be: where significant recommendations are made, have they been accepted by all levels of management and have they been acted upon within a realistic timescale? Where this is not the case, the effectiveness of internal audit is clearly thrown into question, although the reasonableness of management's response will also need to be considered. A reviewer will also want to know if internal audit has given sufficient time for recommendations to be accepted and implemented.

If internal audit does have genuine impact, this will be reflected in its status within the organisation. Service managers will tend to consult and involve such audit sections whenever system changes are under consideration. It will be assumed that audit has both a legitimate interest and a valuable contribution to make. Contrast this to the less effective audit section which is either not consulted, consulted under duress, or consulted because internal rules require that it should be. The status of internal audit should not need to be bolstered by artificial means.

The effectiveness of internal audit's work will be boosted if it is subjected to ongoing quality control review. This may be carried out by management or external audit. Such reviews should be supplemented by client surveys, possibly at the conclusion of each audit. The auditee's view of the auditor can be a very useful measure of the latter's effectiveness, providing appropriate questions are asked of those best placed to give a meaningful response. In this context, the CIPFA audit panel's research study, *The client's view of internal audit*, provides some significant messages.

Conclusion

The performance of internal and external audit may be measured by considering their goals, inputs and processes, but true effectiveness is best gauged by reviewing their output. The range of output measures appears to be relatively narrow. Management and heads of both internal and external audit should have an interest in this topic; particularly the latter. With the onset of competition and contracting out, many organisations and many departments within organisations are looking at alternative arrangements for – or seeking to avoid – audit. It is only by demonstrating genuine effectiveness that the existing providers will survive.

CHAPTER 13
Audit in a competitive environment

The image of the public sector has undoubtedly changed dramatically over the past few years and is certain to emerge as a quite different animal in the next few years. The changes which have occurred will continue and the organisations will be different. That difference is one which primarily affects and is affected by management because management styles will be different and will need to strip away the conventional bureaucracies which many see as the hallmarks of the public sector.

Relationships between the customer and the service provider will need to be addressed where demand and supply, together with quality assurance, may well dictate the terms of the business. That relationship is already being reflected in the move to privatisation and the more commercial approach. Terms such as client, customer, service level agreements, business plans, competitive edge are used, in recognition of the more commercial thinking of the public sector decision-maker and manager.

The change is not just in the styles and attitudes within the public sector but in the impact which other developments are having upon the way in which organisations manage their affairs. What is now apparent is that IT is being regarded as a strategic lever: a means of providing strategic advantage for the services offered by one organisation when competing against others.

Internal audit is not immune from competition. The White Paper, *Competing for Quality*, suggested that all financial services should be opened up for market testing.

Credibility of audit

All organisations concerned with the services they offer recognise that it is crucial to understand the perceptions of customers when trying to identify those areas which need improvement. With this in mind, CIPFA initiated a research project, *The client's view of internal audit*, to focus on how best to enhance and promote audit's role. It was apparent that the success of audit depends upon the credibility of the audit service itself and the commitment of management.

The credibility of audit is the cornerstone of its success. Credibility includes those issues which taken together will point to whether audit is likely to be successful. This will call for attention to be given to the professionalism of audit, the judgement which auditors exercise, its ability to apply a risk-assessment approach to its tasks, a business-like attitude, and having the necessary skills and knowledge.

Professionalism

The APB's *Guidance for Internal Auditors* provides a framework for delivering an effective audit service. It defines internal audit as an independent appraisal function established by the management of an organisation for the review of the internal control system as a service to the organisation. It objectively examines, evaluates and reports on the adequacy of internal control as a contribution to the proper economic efficient and effective use of resources. Adherence to the guidelines will help ensure a professional approach and attitude towards the delivery of an audit service.

Judgement

The auditor who is more concerned with the pennies than the pounds, sees everything in black and white terms and believes that audit enjoys a divine right will inevitably fail in the new competitive environment. The new auditor must be able to demonstrate the right mixture of flexibility, balanced judgement, positive help to the auditee and independence. The auditor must be able to recognise, too, that controls need to be balanced against costs.

Risk assessment

The auditor must be able to identify the risks to the business and then recommend to management the consequences of any of its arrangements which will impact upon the financial well-being of the organisation. This may well take the auditor into discussions on minimum levels of audit cover dependent upon perceived levels of business risk.

Business-like attitude

The consequence of the creation of business-type units within public sector bodies has caused many to look to the compilation of business plans to help formulate their future activities. Audit can usefully explore the benefits of creating its own business plan since the exercise in formulating such a plan is in itself a valuable first step in adopting a more business-like approach. The benefits of business plans for audit are as follows:

1. It is a process for examining the services which can be provided by audit.
2. It pinpoints the potential markets for those services both inside and outside the organisation.
3. It identifies the resources necessary to deliver that level of service.
4. It identifies the costs and charges associated with that service delivery.

Moulding audit into a business unit will demand a culture change for some but it will help those being audited to a better understanding of audit's role and the contribution it can and should be making. This will also cause audit to appreciate more clearly the cost and value of its services.

Skills and knowledge

As a consequence of the nature of audit work, the audit department is likely to be the one unit within an organisation which possesses a wealth of knowledge on the financial systems and procedures throughout the organisation. The systems-based approach to audit, upon which many auditors base their activities, together with the analytical skills which should be the cornerstone of the audit, must give audit the opportunity to demonstrate its contribution to wider management considerations. But audit needs to concentrate its resources on those issues which have substance.

The effect of the competitive environment calls for departments to look to their provision of service and the associated costs. The skills of audit in reviewing such proposals and providing a balanced and independent view has been recognised by several organisations who have called upon audit to appraise their competitive tendering arrangements.

Image

The public sector has, generally speaking, been slow to proclaim its successes and is then surprised when it loses ground. The competitive environment demands a vigorous approach to presenting an image which convinces the customer that there is only one supplier of the service. Audit should be sufficiently confident that it seeks views from its customers, perhaps through regular surveys. It needs too to look carefully at how it presents its findings to management. A badly written and poorly presented report will have little impact and may well result in perfectly valid messages being discarded.

Management's commitment

Obligations

The remit for audit in most public sector organisations lies in statute or recognised practice. For local authorities in England and Wales the Local Government Finance Act 1982 and Accounts and Audit Regulations 1983 require the responsible financial officer to maintain an adequate and effective audit of the accounts of the body. In respect of central government, responsibility for setting internal audit standards and procedures and the professional capability for carrying out and monitoring their implementation were brought together under the Treasury in June 1981.

Status

For audit to provide the necessary service to management it must be independent and be seen to be so. It is difficult, therefore, to understand how some organisations are willing to assign to audit operational functions which conflict with their independence. If audit is to give an independent view on any process, it cannot play any part in the operation of that process. Management must want audit to deliver a high quality product and must then take seriously its findings and recommendations. A consistent failure to act will demoralise staff.

Staffing quality

The success of audit depends largely upon the quality of its staff, and that quality is largely determined by those who appoint the auditors. A lack of commitment by an audit manager invariably affects the morale and performance of the whole audit department. An effective audit manager must believe that he/she has a valuable contribution to make and be able to turn that belief into a reality by delivering results and by securing a general recognition of the value of the work of audit.

Clearly audit must be measurable as a unit of activity, and management must want to assess the performance of that unit just as it should want to assess the successes and failures of other activities. Responsibility for setting the standards against which it must be assessed lies in management's hands. If audit is seen as playing a significant role, other staff will want to join it as a recognised and essential part of their career development.

CHAPTER 14
Tendering for audit services

The environment in which the public sector internal auditor operates is now very competitive and attracts much public attention. The pressure upon internal audit to deliver audit services within an increasingly competitive environment may well encourage auditors and clients to look carefully at the services provided by internal audit and determine the appropriate level of cover which internal audit should provide. The *Competing for Quality* proposals call for internal audit in the public sector to be market tested and this will encourage many more organisations to establish the internal audit section as a trading unit. While the APB guideline suggests that internal audit will always include direct employees of the organisation, as competitive tendering is applied to professional services so internal audit may well be resourced externally. In such circumstances there is a risk that the role of internal audit will be subsumed into a need to adopt a competitive tendering philosophy and insufficient care and attention will be applied to the audit role. It is vital to the success of an in-house internal audit service, therefore, that it not only gets its own house in order, but that it also operates in a business-like manner and is able to bid for work successfully.

The previous chapter, 'Audit in a competitive environment', identified those areas which audit needed to review in order to compete effectively. Before promoting internal audit, the audit manager must be satisfied that a quality product can be delivered. It is also essential to understand the marketplace in which audit operates together with the key changes which are occurring. To this end:

1. Customers need to be identified and their requirements fully understood.
2. The quality of the existing audit service should be evaluated and any shortcomings resolved.
3. A process should be established for marketing internal audit throughout the customer base.

This chapter explores that final stage and discusses three processes to help achieve the objective: business planning, service level agreements and practice accounts.

Business planning

Business planning for audit should help provide a rigour which encourages the audit manager and customer to establish with greater precision what internal audit can contribute to the organisation. Business planning is a process which requires all aspects of the audit section to be examined and should include information to support the existing and proposed level of audit service. Auditors will need to convince senior management that there is a market for their services and the plan should provide the following:

- A description of the demand for the audit service and the arguments as to why the customers will be prepared for the service.
- A statement of the size of the market and its likely growth.
- The extent to which audit will be able to satisfy the customers within that market over a particular period of time and at a particular price.

The business planning process is demanding and will require the audit manager to determine:

- The potential customer base and its demands.
- Any statutory requirements.
- Staffing needs including any special skills.
- Financial information on the cost of the audit service and the charges which will need to be levied.

The intention of the business planning process is for audit to be able to state clearly the extent of its business opportunities. This exercise should, therefore, enable audit management to do the following:

- Ensure that all aspects of the customers' needs are taken into account in any restructuring of the internal audit service.
- Ensure that any statutory responsibilities of internal audit are taken account of in defining customers' needs.
- Provide evidence that internal audit has adopted a systematic approach in defining its services and thus be better able to deliver the promised level of service.
- Help identify the 'core' customer and potential new customers.

Service level agreements

If managers are to control their budgets then they must have control over the costs and deliver the service agreed with the client at the agreed price. Service level agreements (SLAs) are a recognised means of defining the service which the provider agrees to deliver to the client. The SLA will set down the nature of the service, its frequency, and the respective responsibilities of the provider and client. For the SLA to be effective it is important that there is a full understanding by both client and provider of the nature of the service to be delivered. The public sector competitive environment now places more responsibility upon the customer to define requirements but often the customer of audit services is unclear as to the responsibilities of the auditor and the services which the audit section can provide. The auditor must be able, therefore, to market the audit services effectively and ensure that the customer understands precisely what is being provided for the price. A dissatisfied customer will be unlikely to ask for audit services a second time and so it is in the audit manager's interests to ensure that there is no misunderstanding and that satisfaction is assured. Negotiating for added-value work over and above the agreed minimum level of audit coverage will depend upon the continued regard which the customer has for the audit service.

Practice accounts

Practice accounts are a form of trading account to which are debited the costs of the in-house operation and to which are credited the work done at an hourly charge out rate. With practice accounts in place, it will then be possible to monitor expenditure against estimate, income against estimate, staff productivity against planned activity, and actual time taken on audit tasks against planned time. The monitoring is crucial. Establishing practice accounts for their own sake is a worthless exercise and their value is in the management information they provide the audit manager.

The key stages in the establishment of practice accounts are as follows:

- Identifying the aims, objectives and services.
- Identifying all costs.
- Identifying the productive audit time.
- Identifying the work required by customers.
- Producing the business plan in conjunction with senior line management.
- Setting up the account and the monitoring process.
- Preparing an annual report and review of activity for senior management.

The tendering process

The formation of a business plan and practice account will ensure that the audit manager has a clear understanding of the client needs and the required audit resources. As organisations decide to subject their audit services to market testing, so the audit manager must use that information to help prepare for the tendering process. The process involves the following stages:

1. The development of the specification of the quality and extent of the service required by the customer which may either be the whole organisation or just one part of it.
2. The analysis of the specification by internal audit and the preparation and submission of a written proposal by internal audit to provide the required service.
3. The presentation to the customer of audit's tender.
4. The selection of the successful tenderer and awarding of the contract.
5. The monitoring of the service by the customer.

The customer's specification will usually define:

● The area to be audited.
● The nature of the audit activity (e.g. value for money or regularity work).
● The professional standards to which the audit service should adhere (e.g. APB).
● The period of the contract.
● The reporting arrangements.
● The arrangements for tendering.

The written proposal should aim to convince the customer that the tenderer fully understands the customer's needs and provides an assurance that they will receive the best service at the most attractive price. Developing a proposal requires:

● A full understanding of the customer's business.
● A clear understanding of the customer's specification.
● An awareness of the other potential tenderers' strengths.
● A sound assessment of the audit resources required to deliver the level of service.
● The preparation of well presented tender documents for the customer.

The tender documents are critical. Poorly presented and incomplete documents will not convince the customer that the tenderer has the necessary ability and commitment to deliver the required service and so the audit manager must exercise great care in the compilation of the material. Typically the documentation should include the following:

- The identity of the tenderer.
- The nature of the audit approach.
- The extent of coverage.
- The professional standards which will be adhered to.
- The identity of the staff who will be involved in the audit.
- The reporting arrangements.
- The audit fee.

The tender documents will be the primary means of communication with the customer. If the customer is satisfied, the audit manager may well be given the opportunity to make a presentation to the customer and resolve any queries face to face. A structured approach to the presentation of the tender is critical to the success of a tender and, while this will not guarantee success, the audit manager may be assured that a poor undisciplined bid is more likely to result in a lost contract.

PART II

External Audit

CHAPTER 15

General introduction

This second part of the book deals specifically with external audit. Much of what has already been said in the context of internal audit applies to external audit and the differences between the two disciplines relate more to emphasis than to objectives. An external auditor who reads the chapter on the role and objectives of the internal auditor would find little with which to disagree in regard to the external sphere of responsibility. The differences, such as they are, would relate to perspective, accountability, independence and emphasis.

'Perspective' is mentioned because external audit is an independent appraisal function. This obviously adds to independence but has the disadvantage of divorcing the auditor from the internal system of communication and information. Internal auditors who have transferred to external audit often comment that, previously, they knew where the skeletons were but did not have the power to act: now they have the power but do not know where to find the skeletons. However, this wider perspective allows the external auditor to view the organisation from a more detached stance and, as the wider remit covers other organisations, this facilitates comparisons and the percolation of ideas between organisations.

Obviously the external auditor has different lines of accountability from the internal auditor. An internal auditor is primarily responsible to the management within the organisation while the external auditor is a creature of statute and owes a duty to the individual upon whose behalf the audit is being conducted, the taxpayer or consumer, for example.

The additional independence of the external auditor was mentioned earlier. In certain cases this may be eroded, to some extent, by the method by which the auditor is appointed and this varies considerably between types of public sector organisation. An external auditor who is directly appointed by the body under audit, and who holds the appointment at its pleasure, may be more conscious of criticisms of that body than if the appointment had been made independently. Despite this indisputable fact, many public sector bodies continue to be allowed to appoint or have an input into the appointment of their own auditors.

The operational emphasis of internal and external audit is different. The internal auditor concentrates attention upon internal controls within the organisation, with a view to ensuring the security of assets, the reliability of records, economy, efficiency, effectiveness and adherence to policy. Whilst the external auditor is interested in each of these areas and, indeed, devotes a good part of the audit to them, the auditor is also anxious to ensure that the organisation acts only within its statutory powers and that the accounts of the organisation present a fair picture of its activities.

The powers of external auditors – unlike those of internal auditors, which are internally delegated – generally stem from statute. Thus, for example, an external auditor to a local authority will have the broad responsibilities and powers defined by a series of Acts of Parliament. However, these will generally be extended and amplified in a variety of ways – for example, by standards and guidelines issued by employing organisations and professional bodies. Generally speaking, these are extended responsibilities, rather than powers.

The planning and control of external audit work follow many of the same principles as those of internal audit, the major differences being geographical complications and the variety and range of audit undertaken. Techniques differ very little and, indeed, the external auditor will often place reliance upon the tests carried out by internal audit.

The greatest difference between internal and external audit lies, perhaps, in the field of audit reporting. This stems largely from the 'accountability' factor mentioned above. The internal auditor is mainly responsible to management and it is largely to management that the auditor reports. Whilst the external auditor will also report to management, there will also generally be an external reporting function as well. This varies considerably between types of organisation. At the end of the audit, an external auditor is required to provide a certificate for the accounts. Depending upon the results of the audit, this may be a 'qualified' or an 'unqualified' certificate. Where an auditor provides an 'unqualified' certificate it does not necessarily mean that there was nothing amiss. It merely means that the auditor is satisfied that those items which have been found do not materially affect the picture presented by the accounts and there is nothing which it is necessary to draw to the public's attention. Generally the certificate will be accompanied by a report to management (or management letter) drawing attention to those matters which require their attention but which do not merit inclusion as a 'qualification' to the certificate.

In the chapters that follow we will set out in some detail the external audit structure and approach in a number of specific areas of the public sector. Some chapters focus upon specific external audit bodies (the Commission for Local Authority Accounts in Scotland, The Audit Commission for Local

Authorities and the National Health Service in England and Wales, The Local Government Audit Service for Northern Ireland and the National Audit Office). Other chapters describe the overall external audit arrangements for particular parts of the public sector such as education, housing and nationalised and privatised industries.

CHAPTER 16
The Audit Commission

Prior to April 1983, responsibility for the local government audit service in England and Wales rested with the Department of the Environment. The Local Government Finance Act 1982 established a body called the Audit Commission, which assumed responsibility for the local government audit service with effect from 1 April 1983. On 1 October 1990, the statutory external audit function of the National Health Service (NHS) was transferred to the Commission under the provisions of the NHS and Community Care Act 1990.

The Commission, which is independent of central and local government and the NHS, is self-financing, its income coming entirely from fees for audit work. It has two major objectives:

1. To promote the integrity of local government and the NHS by ensuring that authorities spend their money and report their financial situation in accordance with the law and adopt suitable safeguards against fraud and corruption.
2. To promote value for money.

The Commission carries out its work in two principal ways:

1. By appointing auditors to audit the accounts of all local and health authorities in England and Wales and of a variety of other local government and health bodies – for example, joint committees for such purposes as cemeteries, and NHS Trusts.
2. By undertaking studies which make recommendations for improving economy, efficiency and effectiveness of services, and which encourage authorities to learn from one another and apply good management practice which has proved effective elsewhere.

The Commission has a Chairman, Deputy Chairman and up to twenty members drawn from a wide range of interests including industry, local government, the NHS and the accountancy profession. Members are appointed jointly by the Secretaries of State for the Environment, for Health and for Wales, initially for three-year terms. The members meet monthly to determine the broad general policies of the Commission. Although the Commission was established as a new organisation in 1983, the present system of audit and many of the powers currently conferred upon auditors effectively date from 1846 when the Poor Law Unions were established and the District Audit Service was formed.

Scope of work

The duties and responsibilities conferred by the 1982 Act are effectively split two ways – those that are placed upon the Commission, and those placed upon auditors. This section looks in turn at the respective responsibilities of the Commission and its auditors.

The Commission

The principal responsibilities of the Commission are outlined below.

Appointment of auditors

The Commission is responsible for audit appointments to all local authority and NHS bodies. The auditors appointed are either the Commission's own auditors, called District Auditors, or private firms of accountants. At the time of writing 70% of the workload is undertaken by District Auditors, the remainder by eight firms.

The accounts of a wide range of bodies – some 10,000 in all – are audited each year by the Commission's auditors. They consist of the following:

1. Principal local authorities, including counties, metropolitan districts, London boroughs and district councils.
2. Joint authorities and residuary bodies established in 1985 following the abolition of several councils.
3. Parishes and community councils.
4. Committees and joint committees.
5. Health authorities, NHS Trusts and GP fundholders.

Value for money

The Commission seeks to promote value for money in various ways.

Special studies: each year the Commission undertakes a range of special studies. These are designed to determine good management practice in the provision of selected services. Following publication of the central studies, auditors receive detailed audit guides which assist them in identifying improvement opportunities at authorities.

Alongside the studies on major value for money issues, the Commission also carries out detailed evaluations of the effects on local government of various aspects of central government control over its revenue and capital spending. The results, which aim to show what action might be taken by central rather than local government to help local authorities improve their management performance, are sent to the National Audit Office.

The results of Commission studies are always published and are available from HMSO bookshops.

Profiles: to help auditors identify the areas where there appears to be scope for improvement, the Commission prepares annually comprehensive 'Profiles' of each authority. These draw upon the most reliable up-to-date information available centrally and present detailed general, social, demographic and financial statistics relating to the authority. This allows comparisons to be made with a 'family' of broadly similar authorities. It has to be recognised, however, that such comparisons serve only to concentrate audit attention to areas which are worth examining. They do not in themselves provide concrete evidence of any weakness.

Quality Exchange: in 1990 the Commission launched its Quality Exchange as a partnership with local authorities with the following objectives:

- To develop comparative data on a number of indicators of performance and quality, and the processes by which quality might be promoted.
- To provide a contact service enabling authorities to contact each other to share experience and knowledge.
- To provide a data base of information about performance that authorities can use for further research and review.

Information is collected by means of a survey form and subscribers to the scheme receive detailed analyses of the results of the comparative data for each service analysed.

Performance Indicators: The Commission is required by the Local Government Act 1992 to publish a set of performance indicators for local authority services as part of the Citizen's Charter. Every authority in England and Wales will have to record its own performance in these terms, the details will be published in a local newspaper and the Commission will then publish the results nationally. The Commission has identified the five main criteria which the indicators should seek to fulfil:

1. They should be of interest to the citizen.
2. They should, so far as possible, deal with cost, economy and efficiency, as well as with quality and effectiveness.

3. They should support comparisons over time and between authorities.
4. They should deal with the main services provided by local government, and focus on those aspects that reflect the performance of individual authorities.
5. They should be reasonably acceptable.

In addition to its major responsibilities of appointing auditors and undertaking value for money studies, the Commission has a number of other functions.

Preparation of a Code of Practice

The Code is approved by both Houses of Parliament and embodies the Commission's view of best professional practice in terms of audit standards, procedures and techniques. The Code sets out the general duties of auditors and gives guidance on how they should conduct the audit, including sections on independence, professional care, responsibilities to the public, fraud, corruption, value for money and reporting.

Audit fees

The Commission, after consultation with relevant associations and accountancy bodies, must prescribe a scale or scales of fees payable to the Commission in respect of all audits.

Extraordinary audits

In local government the Commission is empowered to direct an appointed auditor to hold an extraordinary audit, either on application by a local government elector for the area of the body or if it appears that it is desirable to do so. The Secretary of State may require the Commission to direct an extraordinary audit if he thinks it desirable in the public interest. Extraordinary audits are infrequent since auditors have the power to examine all of an authority's transactions on a current basis and are not limited to those of any particular year.

Government grants and contracts

The Commission must, on request by any client body, make arrangements for certifying claims on, and contractual payments due from, government departments, and must charge the body a fee to cover the full cost. Grant claim work covers a range of specific grants such as Revenue Support Grant and Housing Subsidy and typically may amount to 12% of time on the main audit. The Commission issues detailed guidance on the audit of particular grant claims following consultation with the government departments concerned, the local authority associations and the accountancy bodies.

Audit of other bodies

The Commission is empowered, with the consent of the Secretary of State, to undertake by agreement the audit of the accounts of bodies other than those required to be audited under the Act, which appear to the Secretary of State to be connected with local government or the NHS. Such audits are relatively few in number.

Auditors

The main responsibilities of the auditor, which are discussed more fully below, are as follows:

1. To give an opinion that the authority's statement of accounts fairly presents its financial position and its income and expenditure for the year (the opinion requirement).
2. To satisfy himself/herself that the authority has made proper arrangements for securing economy, efficiency and effectiveness in its use of resources (the value for money requirement).
3. To consider whether an authority is doing only what it is allowed by law to do (the legality requirement).

The Code of Audit Practice gives more detailed guidance on the conduct of audits, including, in addition to the main duties mentioned above, sections on the auditor's responsibilities in relation to fraud and corruption.

Opinion requirement

The requirement to give an opinion as to whether an authority's statement of accounts presents fairly its financial position has resulted in a change of audit emphasis, with increased attention being given to the verification of final accounts and the operation of the main accounting systems. It has also highlighted some of the inconsistencies and unsatisfactory features of local authority accounting practice, principally in the area of capital accounting. Although accounting practices and financial reporting are based on established traditions, there have been limited statutory requirements or definitive professional guidance as to accounting principles or the form of financial statements. To avoid statutory intervention on this subject by the Department of the Environment, CIPFA took the initiative and prepared a Code of Practice on Local Authority Accounting. This sets out the framework for fair presentation of an authority's financial position.

Value for money requirement

The VFM requirement introduced in the 1982 Act has been met by auditors in a number of ways.

The main thrust of VFM work by auditors has been derived from the Commission's special studies, following the audit guides developed by the Commission. As noted earlier, the special studies seek to identify good practice on a number of issues within a particular area of operation so that individual auditors may compare the performance of their particular authority against good practice yardsticks and, where the comparison is unfavourable, make recommendations for improvements. Generally, the greater proportion of VFM audit time is spent on this aspect.

Auditors may also examine an authority's overall management arrangements, having regard to the authority's strategy, organisational structure and performance monitoring. The Commission has issued guidelines on this type of review, including a diagnostic approach.

The Code of Audit Practice suggests a review of key management areas such as management services, computer services and new technology, workforce management, land and property management, energy and conservation costs, appraisal procedures for new developments, revenue expenditure controls, capital expenditure controls, management of current assets, cash flow and debt management, ordering and tendering, and fixing and reviewing charges for service. Some of these areas have already been addressed in specific Commission special studies.

The development by the Commission of statistical profiles for each authority, as mentioned earlier, enables auditors to highlight services or areas which compare unfavourably and merit further investigation. They can also provide comfort to auditors on the overall economy and efficiency of an authority's operations.

Auditors may undertake local VFM projects and this has long been a feature of audit in England and Wales. Such projects may be based on a cyclical programme or may arise from discussions with the authority or from problems identified during the audit.

The Code stresses that the auditor should not question policy itself, although consideration should be given to the effects of policy and the arrangements by which policy decisions are reached. In practice the distinction between policy and procedures often proves difficult to establish.

Legality requirement

Illegality and loss – local government
Special powers are conferred upon auditors in respect of items of account which are contrary to law and losses caused by wilful misconduct, or a failure to account.

If auditors consider that a local authority is doing, or has done, something for which it has no statutory power, they can apply to the Court for a declaration that the item concerned is unlawful. The Court can agree to or reject the auditor's application for a declaration. If it agrees, it may order the unlawful expenditure to be made good by those responsible for incurring it. If those responsible are members of an authority, and the amount involved exceeds £2,000, the Court may order their disqualification from membership for a specified period. The Court can also order the rectification of the accounts.

If auditors decide there is a loss due to wilful misconduct or failure to account for money or goods, they can themselves order repayment by those concerned (commonly referred to as 'surcharge'). Again, if the person involved is a member of an authority, and the amount involved exceeds £2,000, that person will be disqualified from being a member for a period of five years. In these cases there is a right of appeal against the auditors' decision to either the High Court or the County Court.

With the enactment of the Local Government Act 1988, auditors gained new powers to issue prohibition orders or to apply for judicial review where authorities are contemplating unlawful action. The auditor may issue such an order where he/she believes that an authority or officer is about to do any of the following:

1. Make (or has made) a decision which involves unlawful expenditure.
2. Take (or has taken) a course of action which would be unlawful and cause a loss or deficiency.
3. Enter an unlawful item of account.

In practice, these powers are seldom used, although such cases as there are tend to be given wide publicity. Notwithstanding the infrequency of such cases, auditors are often consulted on matters of legality: the deterrent effect of the powers is considerable.

In the NHS, if auditors find that an authority is taking, or is about to take, illegal action, they may refer the matter by special report to the Secretary of State. There are no powers to refer matters to the Court, nor are there any surcharge powers.

Rights of the public
In local government, members of the public have a number of rights at each audit:

1. Any person interested may inspect and make copies of the accounts and all books, deeds, contracts, bills, vouchers and receipts relating to them.
2. Local government electors or their representatives must be given an opportunity to question the auditor about the accounts.
3. Local government electors or their representatives may attend before the auditor and make objections as to matters on which the auditor could:
   (i) take action for illegality, failure to account or loss through wilful misconduct; or
   (ii) make a report in the public interest.

Apart from the statutory rights of local government electors to question the auditor and to make objections at audit, any person may at any time give information to the auditor which concerns the accounts of a body under audit or is otherwise relevant to the auditor's functions. The auditor will take whatever action appears proper on any information so received and, where appropriate, will remind an informant of the right to make objections to the accounts.

Fraud and corruption

The Code of Audit Practice specifies the auditor's duties in relation to fraud and corruption. Although the auditor no longer has a specific duty to detect fraud, except that which is sufficiently material to distort the financial statements, he/she should be alert to areas particularly exposed to the risk of fraud and advise management accordingly. On corruption, the auditor is required to pay special attention to areas where corrupt practices may be found and ensure that the authority has taken appropriate preventive measures.

Internal organisation and staffing

The Commission is required to appoint a chief officer, known as the Controller of Audit, whose appointment requires the approval of the Secretary of State. The requirement to make the first appointment to this office was, however, reserved to the Secretary of State.

The Commission must appoint such officers and servants as it considers necessary for the discharge of its functions, and at such remuneration or on such terms and conditions as the Commission may determine.

Although the title 'District Auditor' disappeared from the statute book after over a century of use, the Commission has retained the title for its own auditors in deference to tradition and as descriptive of the office. Individual District Auditors continue to be responsible for the audit of the accounts of a number of authorities within a geographical district. A number of persons are assigned to each District Auditor – Senior Managers and Managers – and are responsible to him/her for the conduct of individual audits and for the control and direction of audit staff in the field. At the time of writing there were approximately 1,000 audit field staff allocated between seven audit regions.

In view of the extra workload placed upon auditors by the 1982 Act, the Commission has made greater use of professional firms than hitherto. At the time of writing some 30% of the total work was undertaken by these firms.

Reporting

The Commission and the auditors have separate and distinct reporting responsibilities. These are summarised below.

The Commission

The Commission is required to publish an annual report on the discharge of its functions. Copies are sent to the Secretary of State, who lays copies before each House of Parliament.

As noted earlier, the Commission must undertake studies designed to make recommendations for improving value for money in local government and the NHS. The Commission is required to publish or otherwise make available the results of such studies. Where studies are undertaken into the way in which central government actions impact on value for money in local government, the Commission must also prepare a report, a copy of which is sent to the Comptroller and Auditor General.

Auditors

Auditors have several different reporting requirements placed upon them.

Report in the public interest

If auditors consider that it is in the public interest for them to produce a report, they will do so and send it to the authority. The authority must consider any such report, advertise its availability to members of the public and Press, and respond publicly to the report.

Examples of the kinds of matters which form the subject matter of such reports are:

- The fact that the auditor's opinion on the statement of accounts has been qualified, including conclusions thereon.
- Delayed preparation of accounts.
- Failure to comply with statutory requirements.
- Excessive or inadequate levels of balances, prospective budget deficits etc.
- Failure to achieve economy, efficiency and effectiveness or lack of action on recommendations.
- Weaknesses in management information systems and monitoring arrangements.
- Unnecessary expenditure or loss of income due to waste, extravagance, inefficient financial administration, poor value for money, mistake or other cause.
- High levels of arrears, deficiencies in income collection procedures.
- Objections received at the audit of local authorities and action under sections 19, 20, 25A, 25D of the Local Government Act.
- Misconduct, frauds or special investigations.

Management letters

The auditor is required to summarise in a management letter for members of the authority being audited significant matters that have arisen during the course of the audit. In addition to significant matters arising from the regularity audit, the management letter generally contains a summary of VFM projects and their results and identifies the action taken thereon by officers. It summarises those matters of significance which the auditor has raised during the audit, and the benefits anticipated from implementation of agreed actions. The management letter also provides the agenda for a final meeting which the auditor will seek with members and at which he/she can explain and amplify the nature of any concerns arising and respond to members' questions. In certain cases, authorities must respond publicly to the recommendations contained in management letters.

Auditor's certificate and opinion
When the audit has been concluded, the auditor must enter on the statement of accounts:

1. A certificate that he/she has completed the audit in accordance with the Act.
2. His/her opinion on the statement of accounts.

For authorities not required to prepare a statement of accounts, the auditor's certificate and opinion on the accounts must be entered on the accounts themselves. In general terms, the certificate indicates that all the various audit requirements of the Code of Practice have been carried out, whereas the opinion relates solely to the fair presentation of the financial statements. The words 'presents fairly' were considered more appropriate than the more widely used 'true and fair' principally because of divergencies in local government and the NHS from commercial accounting practices.

The Code also gives advice on the circumstances under which an unqualified audit opinion can be given – these being, broadly, in local government, compliance with the Code of Practice on Local Authority Accounting, adequate disclosure and presentation and compliance with statutory provisions relating to accounts. In practice, there have been relatively few qualified opinions, the most frequent relating to inadequate provisions for bad debts. The opinion requirement has, however, brought into focus some extreme variations in accounting treatment, notably on interest accrual, and the lack of definitive guidance in a number of areas, especially capital accounting.

The National Audit Office (NAO) is the public auditor of central government and should not be confused with the Audit Commission. The NAO is responsible for issuing an audit opinion on the summarised accounts of the NHS and for this purpose it places great reliance on the work of statutory auditors. The Commission and its auditors co-operate closely with NAO to give assurance as to the reliability of the statutory audit work and to safeguard against any unnecessary duplication of work.

CHAPTER 17
The Accounts Commission

The Local Government (Scotland) Act 1973 established the Commission for Local Authority Accounts in Scotland (Accounts Commission), which assumed responsibility for the external audit of local authorities in Scotland with effect from 1 April 1975.

The Commission is an independent body consisting of between nine and twelve members drawn from many walks of life including finance, industry, commerce and academia. It has statutory responsibility for securing the audit of all Scottish local authorities and joint boards; for considering reports arising therefrom; for making recommendations to the Secretary of State and for advising the Secretary of State of any matters relating to local authority accounting referred to them for advice; and for carrying out comparative value for money studies and publishing the results.

To meet its statutory responsibilities the Commission is required to appoint a Controller of Audit, which post also has certain direct statutory duties; this appointment is subject to the approval of the Secretary of State. The Commission may also appoint such other staff as it considers necessary to carry out its functions. In practice this has resulted in a structure under which 50% of the audits are carried out by directly employed staff and 50% by private accountancy firms appointed by the Commission. The Commission's audit staff are divided into four teams based in Glasgow, East Kilbride (Western Area), Glenrothes (Eastern Area) and Inverness (Northern Area). All auditors whether directly employed staff or 'approved auditors' operate independently but under the general direction and supervision of the Controller of Audit. A comprehensive programme of quality reviews is carried out to assess the standard of audit work performed and the Commission draws upon this information when making audit appointments. Audits are rotated at approximately five-yearly intervals.

Bodies audited

The responsibilities of the Accounts Commission embrace the external audit of 9 Regional Councils, 3 Island Councils, 53 District Councils and 21 miscellaneous boards and joint committees. The Islands Councils are multi-purpose authorities, whereas, on the mainland, services are shared between regional councils and district councils. Strathclyde Regional Council is the largest local authority in Britain.

Authorities are required by statute to lodge their unaudited accounts with the Controller of Audit by 31 August following the end of the financial year. Exceptionally, the Secretary of State may grant an extension to an individual authority in the event of its failing to meet the 31 August deadline. Once the audit of the accounts is complete, the auditor has 14 days to provide a certificate to the accounts. That certificate, like its opposite number in England and Wales, is in a format which states that the accounts 'presents fairly' the financial position of the authority.

The work of the Commission is financed entirely by fees paid by local authorities and other bodies calculated to recover the actual cost of their audits on the basis of a standard rate per audit day.

Regularity audit work

One of the primary objectives of the Commission is to ensure that local authorities operate at a high level of probity and accountability. This is reflected in the statutory duties of auditors which state, inter alia, that an auditor:

> shall by examination of the accounts and otherwise satisfy himself that:
> (a) the accounts have been prepared in accordance with regulations and comply with all other enactments and instruments applicable to the accounts;
> (b) proper accounting practices have been observed.

In addition to the statutory responsibilities, auditors have been given guidance regarding the content and nature of their audit in the form of 'Standards and Guidelines' issued by the Commission in 1983 and updated periodically. These cover aspects such as independence; due professional care; planning, controlling and recording; systems appraisal; review of financial statements; auditors' reports and certificates; grant claims, fraud and corruption.

Local authority accounting practice in Scotland is developed under joint arrangements between CIPFA and the Local Authority (Scotland) Accounts Advisory Committee, under the overall approval of the Accounting Standards Board and formal expression in an Accounting Code of Practice. Testing compliance therewith is an important part of auditors' duties as is their responsibility to check that authorities have secured financial systems in place and that they act within their statutory powers.

Value for money responsibilities

These responsibilities fall into three main areas:

1. There is a duty on the Commission to carry out comparative studies and to publish the results.
2. There is a duty on the Commission to develop, and require local authorities to produce and publish, performance indicators.
3. There is a duty on the auditors to satisfy themselves that authorities have made proper arrangements to secure economy, efficiency and effectiveness in the provision of their services.

Comparative studies are undertaken from the Commission's headquarters. For each study a steering group is set up under the chairmanship of the Deputy Controller of Audit (VFM) consisting of local authority practitioners representing the various interest groups concerned with the area under study. The results of each study are published and an audit guide is produced with the objective of enabling auditors to monitor the impact of the study on relevant local authorities and to report back on improved value.

The requirement on the Commission to develop performance indicators derives from The Local Government Act 1992. To discharge its responsibilities thereunder the Commission has developed performance indicators for a range of services, in consultation with local authorities. From 1993/94 each authority will be required to produce these performance indicators and publish them not later than 31 December following each financial year end. The Commission is also required to publish indicators for all authorities. The first set will appear in 1995.

So far as auditors are concerned the statutory duties have manifested themselves in three ways: firstly, in reviewing the arrangements, within authorities, by which management satisfy themselves that economy, efficiency and effectiveness are achieved; secondly, in follow-up work arising from centrally directed studies; and thirdly, as resources permit, in conducting locally determined ad hoc VFM studies. To assist with this, comparative statistics are produced and distributed to auditors from time to time.

Public rights of access

Any 'interested person' may inspect the unaudited accounts at a prescribed time and may, within a prescribed time limit, object to the accounts or any part of them by sending an objection in writing to the auditor and to the Controller of Audit and by sending a copy to the local authority. An objector has a right to be heard by the auditor and has a right to a copy of any statutory report prepared by the Controller of Audit arising from his objection. Unlike his/her counterpart in England and Wales, however, he/she has no right to be advised of the auditor's decision nor any formal right of appeal against that decision. In addition to this statutory objection process, any member of the public can lodge an informal complaint with the Controller's office and this will be accepted for investigation provided it is a valid complaint relating to the financial affairs of a local authority.

Reporting

Auditors report at three different levels:

Management letters
These include references to system weaknesses and other inadequacies which need to be remedied by management. They are submitted to officers of the authority with copies to the Controller of Audit and form part of the material used for quality review purposes. These letters are not public documents.

Reports to audited bodies
Each year auditors report to the authorities on matters which, in their opinion, are worthy of the authorities' consideration or, by virtue of their materiality, require to be brought to members' attention. The authority's chief executive is required to make copies of the report available for public inspection. The auditor sends a copy to the Controller of Audit and this forms one of the principal sources of information which the latter uses to discharge his/her responsibilities.

Certificate to the accounts
The statutory certificate to the accounts is placed on the published abstract of accounts and is a public document.
   Copies of the auditors' annual reports and certificates are submitted to the Commission for their information.

Controller of Audit

The Controller of Audit is the Commission's chief executive with overall responsibility for the management of the Commission's activities. In addition to this general responsibility the Controller has a statutory reporting responsibility in situations where he/she forms an opinion that, arising from the audit, there is:

- an item of account contrary to law; or
- a failure to account for a sum; or
- a loss or deficiency caused by negligence, misconduct or failure to carry out a statutory duty; or
- a debit or credit to the wrong account;

and he/she is not satisfied that remedial action has been or is being taken. In such circumstances, he/she is required to make a 'special' statutory report to the Commission and to forward copies to the authority and to any person who, in his/her opinion, might be affected. In addition the Controller has power to make a statutory report if he/she considers that a matter ought to be reported in the public interest or be drawn to the attention of the Commission or the authority concerned. He/she is also required to report where the Commission requests a report on a particular matter.

Commission's duties

On receiving a statutory report from the Controller of Audit the Commission may in the case of a public interest report – and must if requested to do so in the case of a 'special' report – hold a hearing. Before so doing, the Commission is obliged to seek the observations of the authority and any person to whom a copy of the report was sent. After considering the special report, any observations thereon and matters arising from the hearing, the Commission is required to send the 'special report', together with its findings, to the Secretary of State and may make recommendations to him/her, including surcharge. However, the final decision on surcharge rests with the Secretary of State.

Comparison with the Audit Commission

In so far as value for money activities are concerned, the powers and responsibilities of the Accounts Commission are virtually identical to those of the Audit Commission. In relation to regularity audit there are two main differences: firstly, the Accounts Commission does not have the 'prohibition' powers of the Audit Commission where illegality or loss is thought to be about to arise; secondly, where illegality or loss has arisen this is dealt with in Scotland by the Controller and the Commission, whereas in England and Wales it is the responsibility of individual auditors acting, where appropriate, in conjunction with the Courts.

CHAPTER 18

Local government audit in Northern Ireland

The system of audit of local authorities in Northern Ireland is very similar to the system which operated in England and Wales prior to the establishment of the Audit Commission in 1983. The arrangements are set out in the Local Government Act (Northern Ireland) 1972 as amended principally by the Local Government (Miscellaneous Provisions) (Northern Ireland) Order 1985 and 1992.

The Department of the Environment (NI) appoints local government auditors and a Chief Local Government Auditor who, apart from conducting audits in his/her own right, is responsible for co-ordinating, advising and supervising all other local government auditors.

Unlike England, Wales and Scotland, there are no private firms involved in the external audit of local authorities in Northern Ireland: all auditors are directly employed by the Department. Each auditor is issued by the Department with a warrant which imbues him/her with the necessary authority to conduct the audit and, where necessary, to certify sums due.

The Chief Local Government Auditor is totally independent and is not answerable to any 'quango' although he/she does have a line of responsibility to the Permanent Secretary of the Department of the Environment. The Department can, at any time, direct a local government auditor to carry out an extraordinary audit subject to giving the authority concerned three days' notice.

The audit function extends to 26 district councils, the Northern Ireland Housing Executive which provides a housing service to the whole of the Province, the Fire Authority for Northern Ireland and the Northern Ireland Local Government Officers' Superannuation Committee. The main district council functions are refuse collection, environmental health, building control, leisure, recreation and tourism. The other principal services usually associated with local authorities are conducted by education area boards and health and welfare boards.

Scope of work

The main responsibilities of local government auditors in Northern Ireland are as follows:

1. To certify that the accounts are a true abstract from the books and accounts.
2. To give an opinion on whether or not councils have met the financial objectives specified by the Department of the Environment (NI) for those activities subject to compulsory competitive tendering.
3. To deal with objections from local electors.
4. To deal with items of account contrary to law, failure to account for any sum and losses due to wilful misconduct.
5. To issue prohibition orders where the Local Government Auditor has reason to believe that the council or a council officer is pursuing or is about to pursue a course of action which will result in unlawful expenditure or likely to cause a loss or deficiency or enter an unlawful item of account.
6. To undertake comparative and other studies relating to economy, efficiency and effectiveness.

The audit of accounts duty

There is a statutory duty on the chief financial officer of each authority to make up the accounts of the council at the end of each financial year. The local government auditor is required to give the council not less than 28 days' notice of the day, time and place that he/she has appointed for auditing the accounts and the council is then required to publish that time and place in at least two newspapers circulating in the area not less than 14 days prior to the audit. At least 7 days before the audit the accounts and all books and documents relating thereto have to be deposited for public inspection and copies may be taken.

Having concluded his audit, the local government auditor must report within 14 days and send a copy to the Department together with statement of accounts; the Department then sends a copy to the council. The clerk to the council is required to send copies of the report to all members of the council and lay the report before the next meeting of the council. The clerk of the council must also publish the time and place for inspection by members of the public of the auditor's report by notice in at least one newspaper circulating in the district of the council.

Objections

Any local elector or business ratepayer may be present or may be represented at the audit and may make an objection to the accounts. The auditor can require that objection to be put in writing.

An aggrieved objector may, within 6 weeks of the auditor's decision require him/her to state, in writing, the reasons for the decision. The objector then has a right of appeal to the Court against the auditor's decision. Where the Court considers that the auditor's decision is wrong in respect of an appeal by an objector, it may reverse that decision and make an order for repayment against those responsible for the transaction in question.

Illegality, failure to account and losses

Where a local government auditor forms the view that any item of account is contrary to law he/she may apply to the Court for a declaration to that effect. The only exception to this is where an item of account has been sanctioned by the Department.

Where the Court agrees with the auditor, it may make the declaration and may make an order requiring any person or persons responsible for incurring or authorising the unlawful expenditure to repay it in whole or in part to the council, having regard to all the circumstances including the individual's means and ability to repay. Where such expenditure exceeds £2,000 and the person responsible is a council member the Court may order disqualification for a specified period. The Court may also order rectification of the accounts in such cases.

There is an important caveat, however, that the Court shall not make an order for repayment or disqualification where it believes that the person responsible acted reasonably or in the belief that he/she was acting within the law.

The procedure for dealing with failure to account for a sum or a loss or deficiency due to wilful misconduct is somewhat different. Where an auditor forms such an opinion he/she is required to certify that the sum or the loss or deficiency is due from the person or persons responsible. Either the auditor or the council may then recover that sum for the benefit of the council. Any person subject to a certification has a right of notification in writing from the auditor of the reasons for the decision and may appeal the case to the Courts. Where the amount exceeds £2,000 and the person responsible is a council member, there follows automatic disqualification from being elected or acting as a member for five years.

Studies relating to economy, efficiency and effectiveness

A duty was introduced in 1985 to the effect that the auditor, at the request of the Department of the Environment, shall carry out comparative and other studies designed to enable him/her to make recommendations for improving economy, efficiency and effectiveness in the provision of council services. There is, however, a requirement for the Department of the Environment to consult with various representative bodies and associations before commissioning any study.

Reporting

As mentioned above, the auditor is required, within 14 days of completion of the audit, to send a copy of the auditor's report together with the statement of accounts to the Department. The Department then provides the council with a copy of the auditor's report and certified accounts.

Reports following studies into economy, efficiency and effectiveness must be published or otherwise made available by the Department of the Environment, together with any recommendations made by the auditor, as a result of the studies.

CHAPTER 19
The National Audit Office

Introduction

The National Audit Act 1983 created the National Audit Office (NAO) with the Comptroller and Auditor General (C&AG) as its head. The C&AG and the NAO are totally independent of government. The C&AG certifies the accounts of all government departments and a wide range of other public sector bodies, and has statutory authority to report to Parliament on the economy, efficiency and effectiveness with which departments and other bodies use their resources.

History of the National Audit Office

The first Comptroller General of the Exchequer was appointed in 1314 and successive audit bodies were established and re-established over the next 500 years. The present office of Comptroller and Auditor General (C&AG) was created by the Exchequer and Audit Departments Act of 1866, following the major Parliamentary and public sector reforms in the nineteenth century.

Although the statutory framework for public audit in the United Kingdom remained broadly unchanged for over a century, the content of the audit itself advanced in a number of significant ways. The most important development was the increasing emphasis given to value for money investigations into questions of economy, efficiency and, more recently, effectiveness. Although this aspect of the work was non-statutory, it has been a significant part of the C&AG's responsibilities for at least the last 30 years.

In recent years there has been an increasing demand for greater public and Parliamentary accountability for all bodies receiving public funds. This has been reflected in a succession of Parliamentary reviews into the scope of the C&AG's responsibilities and the nature of the work. These reviews culminated in an inquiry in 1980 by the Committee of Public Accounts, which recommended important developments in the status and functions of both the

C&AG and the C&AG's staff. The National Audit Act 1983 contained a number of these recommendations.

National Audit Act 1983

The National Audit Act 1983 reinforced the C&AG's financial and operational independence from the Executive and brought a closer relationship with Parliament. It created the National Audit Office with the Comptroller and Auditor General as its head. It established a clearer framework for access to departments and many other bodies receiving public funds. It also provided the statutory authority for the C&AG's work on economy, efficiency and effectiveness.

The Comptroller and Auditor General

The C&AG's full title is 'Comptroller General of the Receipt and Issue of Her Majesty's Exchequer and Auditor General of Public Accounts'. As *Comptroller General*, he/she authorises the issues of public funds to government departments and other public sector bodies. As *Auditor General*, his/her statutory duties are to certify the accounts of all government departments and a wide range of other public bodies; to examine revenue and store accounts; and to report the results of the examinations to Parliament. He/she also has statutory powers to carry out and report to Parliament on examinations of economy, efficiency and effectiveness in the use of resources by those bodies he/she audits or to which he/she has rights of access.

The C&AG's work provides independent information, advice and assurance to Parliament and the public about all aspects of the financial operations of government departments and many other bodies receiving public funds. This is an important link in the chain of accountability and stewardship of public funds.

Independence of the C&AG

The C&AG is wholly independent of the Executive. The office is subject to certain broad financial controls by Parliament but not to its operational or professional control. Constitutionally and by statute, the C&AG enjoys a high degree of independence, as evidenced by the following:

1. The Comptroller is appointed by the Queen by Letters Patent on an address from the House of Commons moved by the Prime Minister after agreement with the Chairman of the Committee of Public Accounts.
2. The Comptroller can be removed from office only by the Queen on an address from both Houses of Parliament.
3. The Comptroller's salary is paid directly from the Consolidated Fund without requiring the annual approval of the Executive or of Parliament.

4. The Comptroller appoints his/her own staff and determines their number, salaries and conditions of service.
5. The Comptroller alone decides on the examinations to be carried out, the extent and conduct of such investigations and the content of any reports.

Relationship with Parliament

By virtue of the office, the C&AG is an officer of the House of Commons, whose main duties are carried out on behalf of Parliament and in close association with the Committee of Public Accounts. Most of the Committee's investigations are based on the C&AG's reports on economy, efficiency and effectiveness; and the C&AG takes into account any proposals from the Committee when deciding the programme of examinations the C&AG's staff should undertake.

The expenses of the NAO are met by moneys voted by Parliament. The annual budget is presented for Parliamentary approval by the Public Accounts Commission, a body set up under the 1983 Act whose members are all Members of the House of Commons. The Commission also appoints the Accounting Officer for the NAO's annual accounts and an independent auditor for those accounts. The Commission reports periodically on its activities to the House of Commons.

Scope of work

The Comptroller and Auditor General's audit responsibilities

The C&AG has certain duties enjoined by statute, principally concerned with the annual examination of accounts. In addition, discretionary powers are available to carry out other examinations and report the results. There are also limitations in the scope and nature of the work:

1. *The C&AG must:*
   (a) audit and certify the appropriation accounts of all government departments;
   (b) audit the revenue accounts;
   (c) examine departmental store accounts;
   (d) audit and certify other accounts, including those of Executive Agencies, as laid down by the Exchequer and Audit Departments Acts and other statutes;
   (e) report as necessary to Parliament on the results of these audits.
2. *The C&AG may:*
   (a) audit and certify other accounts by agreement;
   (b) have rights of access to a wide range of bodies where he/she is not the appointed auditor but which are largely financed by public funds;

   (c) examine the economy, efficiency and effectiveness of expenditure and the use of resources by bodies where he/she is appointed auditor or has rights of access, either under statute or by agreement;

   (d) report to Parliament on the results of these examinations.

3. *The C&AG does not:*

   (a) formally disallow expenditure, or give judgements or rulings on questions of legality;

   (b) audit or have access to the accounts of nationalised industries or local authorities;

   (c) have a general power to 'follow public money wherever it goes' with rights of access to companies, organisations or individuals receiving grants, subsidies or other assistance from public funds;

   (d) question the merits of policy objectives when carrying out examinations of economy, efficiency and effectiveness;

   (e) examine questions of maladministration by departments affecting individual members of the public. (This is the field of the Parliamentary Commissioner for Administration.)

Audit of accounts

The C&AG is the appointed auditor for some 500 public sector accounts, with a combined expenditure and revenue of over £450 billion. This is clearly a major task. The certification of these accounts is based upon a financial and regularity audit which enables the provision of annual assurance of the following:

1. The form and content of the accounts conform to statutory and Treasury requirements.
2. The figures in the accounts are properly stated.
3. The funds have been applied to the services and for the purposes intended by Parliament.
4. The payments and receipts are in accordance with Parliamentary authority, statute and other regulations.

The audit standards, approach and methods adopted for the C&AG's certification audit are in all significant respects similar to those applied within the audit profession generally. Planning, monitoring and review procedures are directed towards achieving a cost-effective audit carried out to a high professional standard.

Computers

Computer technology is changing rapidly and the NAO is continuing to develop and adapt its audit methods and techniques to meet the challenges posed. Examination of computer-based systems is undertaken by audit staff with support from specialists in information technology where required.

Internal audit

In planning and carrying out its certification audits, the NAO evaluates the scope for making as much use as possible of relevant work undertaken by internal audit, by assessing the standards and coverage of that work and reviewing the results.

The C&AG has encouraged developments to help raise standards of internal auditing in central government and to promote the importance of its role by a policy of fostering the development of internal auditing and – while retaining the respective independence of the parties involved – promoting co-ordinated audit coverage in order to achieve the most effective use of total audit resources.

Accounts audited by the C&AG

The C&AG examines and certifies the accounts of government departments and a wide range of public corporations, agencies and other public bodies, through which flows over 60% of public expenditure. In addition, the C&AG is the appointed auditor for 41 United Nations and other international accounts.

The accounts audited vary widely in type, size and complexity.

Appropriation and Revenue accounts

There are 169 of these, produced by government departments to account for the use of money voted by Parliament and the receipt of revenue by the Inland Revenue and Customs and Excise.

National Loans Fund accounts

These, of which there are 27, are for drawings from and repayments to the National Loans Fund in respect of the funding of nationalised industries and public corporates.

White Paper accounts

There are 139 such accounts, audited under statutes other than the Exchequer and Audit Departments Acts and laid before the House of Commons.

Executive Agency accounts

There are 5 of these. Many agencies are financed directly by money voted by Parliament. In addition to accounting for these moneys through appropriation accounts, such agencies will also have to produce separate financial statements, normally on an accrual basis, to be audited by the C&AG. The remaining agencies are (or will be) established as Trading Funds and audited by the C&AG under the Government Trading Funds Act 1973, as amended by the Government Trading Act 1990. These agencies will produce full commercial style accounts.

Other UK accounts

There are 85 other UK accounts, audited primarily by agreement and not usually laid before Parliament.

Internal accounts

There are 41 of these, audited by agreement and presented to governing bodies.

Value for money audit

The NAO's VFM audit field covers annual cashflows in excess of £450 billion and assets of much greater value. It is more extensive than the certification audit field as NAO have access rights to a number of bodies in receipt of public funds without the corresponding certification audit responsibilities. The NAO also have VFM access rights to bodies under s. 6 and 7 of the National Audit Act.

A more detailed booklet, *A Framework for Value for Money Audit*, can be purchased from the National Audit Office, Buckingham Palace Road, London SW1W 95P. An outline of the VFM work undertaken is set out below.

The main objective of the C&AG's value for money audit is to provide independent information, advice and assurance to Parliament about economy, efficiency and effectiveness in the use of resources in the departments and other organisations examined. A secondary objective is to identify ways of improving value for money and to encourage and assist audited bodies to improve systems and controls. The audit is carried out over a planned cycle and is directed towards establishing the following:

1. That proper arrangements exist for securing economy, efficiency and effectiveness. Particular attention is paid to areas where the largest resources are involved and the risks are greatest, and to the main control and management information systems.
2. That those systems are operating satisfactorily in practice. This requires a selective examination of important projects and programmes.

The NAO define economy, efficiency and effectiveness as follows:

1. *Economy* is concerned with minimising the cost of resources used for an activity, having regard to appropriate quality.
2. *Efficiency* is concerned with the relationship between the output in terms of goods, services or other results and the resources used to produce them. How far does the activity achieve the maximum output for a given input or use the minimum input for a given output?
3. *Effectiveness* is concerned with the relationship between the intended impact and the actual impact of an activity. How far do the outputs in terms of goods, services or other results achieve the effects that were needed? How far do they achieve policy objectives?

Typical areas for NAO value for money audit include the following:

1. Privatisations.
2. Financial and contractual control over major capital works projects and associated areas.
3. Provisioning and procurement systems for equipment, stores, transport and other services.
4. Control and utilisation of fixed assets and other resources.
5. Costs of administration and services.
6. Control and utilisation of human resources.
7. Effectiveness of grants, subsidies, loans, agricultural and industrial support and overseas aid.
8. Collection of revenue.
9. Implementation of major programmes and projects in health, education and social fields.

The nature of VFM investigations falls into four broad categories:

- *Selective investigations* of signs of possible serious waste, extravagance, inefficiency, ineffectiveness or weaknesses in control. These are largely confined to examining whether criticism is justified, examining causes and considering action taken or needed to introduce improvements: for example, finding out why a weapon system overran its costs or timetable or failed to meet the requirements for which it was designed and developed; and discovering how far the lessons learnt are being applied to future projects.
- *Major broad-based investigations* of a whole audited body or of important activities, projects or programmes. These are designed to lead to reports giving assurance in major areas where arrangements are found to be satisfactory and no criticism is justified, as well as drawing attention to material weaknesses in control or achievement and their consequences: for example, investigating the implementation and results of the various schemes which form the Government's programme for reducing or alleviating unemployment.

- *Major reviews* of standard managerial operations which tend to follow common patterns or procedures or established good practice. Areas for such 'good housekeeping' examinations include stores procurement, maintenance of buildings or equipment, operation of transport fleets, etc.
- *Smaller-scale investigations*. These are not normally expected to lead to a report to Parliament but are directed towards producing useful improvements in value for money, strengthening systems and fostering cost-consciousness.

The general aim is to secure a 'mixed diet' of investigations and reports, covering each of the first three categories above. Some examinations pursue matters within a single department while 'across the board' studies follow up a particular subject or function – for example, investment appraisal or control of building maintenance – across a number of different departments.

The major studies have emphasised lessons to be learned as a means of improving management in the future; and the clear demonstration of weaknesses for follow-up by Parliament has produced significant benefits. The firm audit evidence underlying these reports has promoted a necessary authority and impact in dealing with difficult and complex issues.

The planning and execution of value for money examinations include the following:

1. The preparation and annual updating of strategic audit plans, looking up to four years ahead.
2. The preparation of detailed plans for the year ahead, based on the strategic plans and establishing aims, approach and timetables for individual studies and associated staff needs.
3. Preliminary and full investigations.
4. Consideration of the lessons for the future from each completed examination.

NAO value for money examinations avoid questioning the merits of policy objectives, which are for Ministers and Parliament to decide. This does not preclude, however, an examination of the completeness and accuracy of the information on which those decisions are based, nor does it prevent an investigation of the implementation of agreed policy and its impact.

Internal organisation and staffing

The Comptroller and Auditor General is head of the National Audit Office. NAO policy, planning and overall operations and management are considered by a senior management group. This comprises the C&AG, the Deputy C&AG and the Assistant Auditors General who are the principal advisers, and the Director of Corporate Policy. The power of final decision rests with the C&AG.

The main body of the Office comprises four line audit units, each headed by an Assistant Auditor General responsible for the audit of individual departments and other bodies. A central unit is responsible for: personnel, administration, finance and training; guidance on audit standards and methods and research; policy and planning; and information technology.

The senior management and the majority of staff are located at the NAO's London headquarters. There are overseas offices dealing with United Nations and other international accounts. Staff in both UK and overseas locations travel widely in carrying out local audits of smaller departments and outstations.

The NAO employs some 850 audit, specialist, and supporting staff. Over 300 are professional accountants, most of whom are members of the Chartered Institute of Public Finance and Accountancy.

The Office also employs specialist advisers in such disciplines as economics and operational research. There are also secondments and exchanges with staff from government departments, leading firms of professional accountants and from overseas. The NAO recruits good honours graduates from a wide range of disciplines. Unless they have relevant degrees, all recruits undertake a conversion course in economics, company and business law, financial accounting and auditing, and financial decisions-making. They are then required to train for three years to acquire a full professional accountancy qualification with the Institute of Chartered Accountants in England and Wales. The Office has up to 130 trainees under professional training at any one time.

Professional training is supplemented by an in-house training programme. Practical experience and training on the job, under the supervision of Audit Managers and other staff, are an integral part of the professional development of new entrants.

For experienced and more senior staff, there is a programme of continuing professional education to help ensure that they keep up to date with the latest audit techniques and developments.

Reporting

In addition to certifying and reporting on the accounts audited, the C&AG reports to Parliament the main results of the value for money examinations. In some circumstances – as in the audit of the accounts of the United Nations agencies – the C&AG reports to the governing bodies of the organisations concerned.

The C&AG's reports are highly selective. Many matters arising from certification and value for money audits are raised and resolved satisfactorily with the audited bodies without the need for a formal published report.

The form of the C&AG's reports is not prescribed. There is complete discretion to decide on their timing and content. They are always discussed with the audited bodies before publication to ensure that the facts are complete and fairly presented. The reports normally incorporate their replies to the matters raised and set out action taken. The final decisions on the report content always rest with the C&AG.

The C&AG always reports on any qualifications of the audit opinion. There is also a requirement to report each year on the results of the examination of revenue and store accounts under the Exchequer and Audit Departments Acts.

The bulk of the C&AG's reports, however, are concerned with the results of the value for money examinations. In the decision as to whether and what to report, the main factors taken into account include the following:

1. The size, nature and general importance of the subject.
2. The areas and issues which the Committee of Public Accounts are likely to find most rewarding for their enquiries.
3. The nature and extent of any failings in control, the reasons, and the financial effects.
4. The extent to which the particular case illustrates wider weaknesses in systems of financial information and control, affecting other projects or programmes.
5. How far any weaknesses have already been recognised or accepted by the audited body concerned, the corrective action taken or proposed, and how effective this seems likely to be in establishing sound financial control.

Generally the C&AG feels free to include in the report all matters on which he/she considers Parliament should be informed. But he/she does not in practice disclose certain information classified on security grounds or advice given to Ministers by their departments. Nor is there an attempt to second-guess either policy or commercial decisions, though notice may be brought to the basis for – or financial and other consequences of – such decisions.

Reports resulting from the C&AG's annual certification audit are normally published with the related accounts when these are certified and presented to Parliament between July and October each year. The C&AG's other reports to Parliament are published regularly throughout the year.

The Committee of Public Accounts

The Committee of Public Accounts was established in 1861 and is the senior Parliamentary Select Committee dealing with financial matters.

Under House of Commons standing orders all accounts certified by the C&AG and submitted to Parliament are referred to the Committee for examination, together with the related C&AG's reports. In practice, the Committee concentrates largely upon pursuing those matters included in the C&AG's reports, seldom examining the details of the accounts themselves.

The Committee has up to 15 members. It is chaired by a senior member of the Opposition, normally an ex-Minister with relevant financial experience. The Committee does not concern itself with the merits of policy objectives, conducting its business on non-party political lines. It meets twice a week throughout most of the Parliamentary session, and takes evidence primarily from the Accounting Officer (the permanent head) of the audited department concerned.

The Committee submits reports to Parliament throughout the year on the results of its enquiries, with recommendations for further action. The Government responds to each report in a published Treasury Minute, giving information on the steps taken to implement the Committee's recommendations and to apply the wider lessons learned. The Committee may in turn follow up this subsequent action. The Committee's reports and the Treasury Minutes are also debated once a year on the floor of the House of Commons.

The close co-operation which exists between the C&AG and the Committee of Public Accounts, within their respective independence, was endorsed by a former chairman of the Committee in the following terms: 'The C&AG's effectiveness largely depends on the fact that his reports are considered and followed through by the Committee; the Committee's effectiveness on the fact that it has his reports as a starting point.'

These mutual benefits have been consolidated and developed. The C&AG consults the Committee on the main features of the forward work programme – mainly in the value for money field – and, in making decisions, takes into account any view or proposals the Committee may put forward. The Committee may in turn offer advice to the Public Accounts Commission on its examination of the NAO's annual budget.

CHAPTER 20

Education

Public sector education is increasingly being provided independently of local education authorities and, as education providers become independent, so different external audit regimes are being adopted. The primary providers of education in the public sector are, now:

- the local education authorities;
- the Department for Education in respect of Grant Maintained (GM) schools;
- the Further Education Funding Council (FEFC) in respect of colleges of further education (such as Sixth Form Colleges and Technical Colleges, for example); and
- the Higher Education Funding Councils (HEFC) in respect of universities and other higher education institutions.

Local education authorities (LEAs)

The external audit of LEAs is undertaken by the Audit Commission for England and Wales and by the Accounts Commission for Scotland. These audits are arranged as part of the normal audit arrangements of the respective local authorities under the terms of the respective Commissions' statutory arrangements.

Grant Maintained schools

The Education Reform Act 1988 provided for primary and secondary schools to opt out of LEA control and to be directly grant aided by the Department for Education (DFE). A detailed external audit code for the GM schools sector was issued by the DFE in July 1992 and it set down the arrangements for the scope of the audit, the procedures for the selection of external auditors and requirements for reporting.

Scope of the audit

The Code states that the coverage of the audit will need to be sufficient to enable the auditors to form an opinion as to whether:

- the financial statements give a true and fair view of the state of affairs of the school;
- the financial statements have been properly prepared in accordance with the Financial Reporting and Annual Accounts Requirements documents issued by the DFE;
- proper accounting records have been kept;
- pension contributions payable to the Teachers' Pension Scheme have been paid in accordance with the scheme; and
- the school's systems of internal controls were such as to comply with the obligations placed on the governing body by the Secretary of State and any material weaknesses were identified in them.

An appendix to the code provides a detailed questionnaire for a first term survey of internal controls.

Qualifications of auditors

The code states that an audit of a grant maintained school may be undertaken by either:

(i) the Audit Commission; or
(ii) those accountants who are members of one of the professional accountancy bodies which are recognised supervisory bodies and who are also registered to audit limited companies; or
(iii) those people or bodies approved by the DTI to audit limited companies or approved by the DFE to audit GM schools. (At the time of writing the only body so approved is CIPFA whose regulations for approving such auditors parallel closely the regulatory regime established for the registration of auditors of companies under the Companies Act 1989. Members of CIPFA who are qualified by the DFE to carry out the audit of a GM school are then known as 'registered GM school auditors'.)

Reporting

The code defines what should be contained in the auditor's report and then requires the auditor to send a copy of the management letters and audit reports to the DFE and to the school.

Colleges of further education

The chief executive of the FEFC is accountable to Parliament for:

(i) ensuring that public funds are safeguarded;
(ii) securing value for money (VFM) from public funds; and
(iii) monitoring colleges' compliance with any terms and conditions attached to their funding.

To fulfil these responsibilities whilst avoiding an excessive audit burden on colleges, the chief executive will rely, to a large extent, on the audit work carried out by colleges' external auditors. For this reason, the FEFC has an interest in the selection process by which these auditors are appointed and in the appointments themselves.

Scope of the external audit

The basic objective of the college's external auditors is to report on the truth and fairness of the financial position of the college and any subsidiary companies shown in the financial statements. If the college is a limited company, the Companies Act requires the auditor also to form an opinion as to whether proper accounting records have been kept, whether the accounts are in agreement with those records, and to state that the accounts comply with the disclosure requirements of the Companies Act. In addition, where public money and other income restricted in its use is involved, the scope of the auditors' report must be extended for all colleges to cover the 'regularity' of transactions. It is likely also that the FEFC will require the colleges to have the accuracy of certain of their statistical returns to the FEFC certified by their external auditors.

Qualification of external auditors

The FEFC issued guidance to help colleges intending to be incorporated as further education corporates under Sections 15 and 16 of the Further and Higher Education Act 1992 to select and appoint their external auditors. The guidance is also for colleges to be designated by the Secretary of State under Section 28 of the Act. The guidance states that the external audit of a college may be undertaken by:

(i) those accountants who are registered to audit limited companies in accordance with Part II of the Companies Act 1989 and who are chartered accountants, certified accountants or Authorised Public Accountants; or

(ii) the Audit Commission for Local Authorities and the National Health Service in England and Wales; or

(iii) partners in public practice who are members of the Chartered Institute of Public Finance and Accountancy.

If the college is itself a company limited by guarantee or has subsidiary companies that are incorporated then it will be necessary for the Audit Commission or the CIPFA partner to make suitable arrangements to comply with the Companies Act.

Audit approach

While each audit firm (including the Audit Commission) has its own approach to carrying out audits, all will follow broadly the following stages:

1. A pre-audit (first year only) to enable the auditors to familiarise themselves with the college.
2. An interim visit to review and test the main accounting systems (e.g. budgetary control, management information, salaries, payments to suppliers, bank accounts, income).
3. A final visit to audit the balance sheet and income and expenditure account, and to review the financial statements and the notes which accompany them.
4. The giving of an audit opinion on the financial statements.
5. The submission of a management letter to the board of governors which reports any weaknesses in controls identified during the audit and recommends how they may be remedied.

Irregularities, including fraud

The board of governors of the college is responsible for ensuring the establishment and maintenance of an adequate system of internal control which includes controls for the prevention and detection of irregularities and fraud. External auditors have a duty to plan and conduct their audit so that there is a reasonable expectation of detecting material mis-statements in the accounts resulting from irregularities, including fraud, or breaches of regulations. However, they do not have a duty to search specifically for irregularities and fraud and their audit should not, therefore, be relied upon to disclose them.

Reporting arrangements

The external auditors' examination normally culminates in two types of report: a formal opinion on the financial statements and a management letter.

Auditors should provide a management letter within one month of issuing their opinion on the annual financial statements and it should be addressed to the board of governors through the audit committee. The management letter should include any significant matters arising out of the audit which might lead to material errors or impact on future audits, or where, for example, economies could be made or resources used more efficiently. It should also recommend improvements, particularly in the following areas:

• weaknesses in the structure of accounting systems and internal control;
• deficiencies in the operation of accounting systems and internal control including internal audit;
• inappropriate accounting policies and practices;
• non-compliance with legislation, accounting standards, and other regulations; and
• matters raised in previous management letters where remedial action remains incomplete.

Final versions of management letters, including those arising from an interim audit and other reports of audit findings should be forwarded to the chief auditor at the FEFC by the external auditor at the same time as the original goes to the college. In the same way colleges should send a copy of their reply to the chief auditor at the FEFC.

Serious weaknesses or an accounting breakdown should be reported without delay to the principal, the chairman of the board of governors, the chairman of the audit committee and the director of finance at the FEFC.

Higher education institutions

The HEFCs for England and Wales and Scotland are responsible for issuing guidance to help higher education institutions select and appoint their external auditors. This guidance will be contained in Audit Codes of Practice and their provisions must be adhered to by higher education institutions as a provision of the settlement of grant arrangements.

The responsibilities of the HEFCs are broadly similar to those of the FEFC.

Qualification of external auditors

The qualifications required for external auditors of higher education corporations are set out in schedule 7 of the Education Reform Act 1988. Other higher education institutions should ensure that their auditors are eligible for appointment as external auditors under the provisions of the Companies Acts.

The governing body of the institution is usually responsible for appointing external auditors and it should determine the selection criteria and procedures, taking into account the guidance given by the HEFC prior to receiving proposals. Particular attention should be given to such issues as the quality of service (including experience) and audit fees, including a clear basis and commitment on future fee increases.

Institutions will need to reappoint their auditors formally each year.

Additional services

The Scottish HEFC's Code provides for institutions to ask external auditors to provide additional services beyond the scope of the statutory audit, including special investigation work, taxation compliance and advice. Where an accountancy firm is contracted to provide internal audit services, this will preclude the firm from also providing external audit services. Institutions are required to disclose fees paid to its external auditors for other services. The situation for England and Wales was not determined at the time of writing.

Reporting arrangements

External audit should report, by way of a management letter within two months of issuing an opinion on the financial statements, any significant matters arising from the audit. In order to provide the HEFC Chief Executive with assurance on compliance with the financial memorandum, the institution's audit committee must send copies of the external auditor's management letters together with any response immediately after the letter has been considered by the audit committee of the institution.

Auditors must report serious weaknesses, significant frauds or any major accounting breakdown without delay to the chairman of the Governing Body, the chairman of the audit committee, and the Chief Executive of the HEFC. The institution must also report without delay other serious weaknesses, significant frauds or major accounting breakdowns which come to light other than through external auditors' work. Information obtained, suitably anonymised, will be disseminated throughout the sector by HEFC, thereby enabling institutions to take whatever action they consider necessary to protect their interests.

A serious weakness is regarded by the HEFC's external audit code as one that may result in a significant fraud or loss. Significant fraud is taken to mean a fraud where one or more of the following factors are involved:

1. The sums of money are in excess of £10,000.
2. The particulars of the fraud are novel, unusual or complex.
3. There is likely to be great public interest because of the nature of the fraud or the people involved.

Reporting

The external auditors are required to report on the following:

  (i) Do the financial statements give a true and fair view of the state of the institution's affairs and of its income and expenditure and statement of cashflow for the year, taking into account relevant statutory and other mandatory disclosure and accounting requirements, and HEFC requirements?

 (ii) Have funds from whatever source administered by the institution for specific purposes been properly applied to those purposes and, if relevant, managed in accordance with relevant legislation?

(iii) Have funds provided by the HEFC been applied in accordance with the Financial Memorandum and any other terms and conditions attached to them?

(iv) Do the financial statements comply with the Companies Acts where the institution is incorporated under the Companies Acts?

CHAPTER 21
Housing

The primary providers of public sector housing are local authorities and housing associations. While the former were once active in building new dwellings, restrictions on such investment has meant that housing associations are now emerging as the new public sector housing developer. In addition, some local authorities are transferring their housing stocks to housing associations and this is also helping to increase the size of the housing association market.

Legal status of housing associations

The legal definition of a housing association was set down in the Housing Act 1957 and subsequently amended by the Housing Association Act 1985. The objective of a housing association is broadly to provide accommodation for those who would otherwise be living in unsatisfactory conditions, and to achieve this they have to acquire and/or modernise dwellings and then manage and maintain them.

The legal status of housing associations depends upon the particular statute under which they were created. An association may, for example, be a society, body of trustees or a company and be regarded as:

- a housing association registered with the Housing Corporation;
- 1965 Act Society (as registered with the Registrar of Friendly Societies);
- a charitable housing association (which is a registered charity but not an exempt charity under the terms of the Charities Act 1960);
- an association with charitable status (which is a registered charity or a 1965 Act Society which is exempt under the terms of the Charities Act 1960);
- a co-ownership society;
- an almshouse; or
- a self-build society.

Housing associations can be legally constituted in various ways but only those associations who are registered with the Housing Corporation may receive loans, grants and subsidies payable under the Housing Acts. The only types of associations which may be registered with the Housing Corporation are 1965 Act Societies and charitable housing associations. The 1965 Act Societies are obliged to follow:

(i) their rules as registered with the Registrar of Friendly Societies;
(ii) the Industrial and Provident Societies Acts; and
(iii) various Housing Acts.

The Housing Corporation was established by statute in 1964 and its powers have been extended by subsequent Acts of Parliament. Guidance on the running of housing associations (of which there are now over 3,000) is provided by the Corporation which is responsible for registering associations, funding their activities (providing 85% of their finances) and exercising a regulatory function.

Others closely involved in the activities of housing associations include the Department of the Environment, the National Federation of Housing Associations (NFHA) which provides services to associations and the Institute of Housing which provides advice and guidance to those managing the associations.

Accounting issues

Accounting requirements for registered housing associations are set down in the Registered Housing Associations (Accounting Requirements) Order 1982 (SI 828) and further detailed in the *Recommended Form of Published Accounts for Housing Associations* published by the Housing Corporation and NFHA. The overriding requirement is that the accounts must reflect a 'true and fair view' as required by the Companies Act, and, where there is any necessity to depart from the 1982 Order in order to give such a view, the reasons must be noted in the accounts.

Auditing requirements

The accounts of housing associations must be audited in accordance with the Companies Act, Housing Acts and Housing Association Act. In addition, various statutory returns must be provided to the relevant registrars under the Industrial and Provident Societies Act 1965 and the Friendly and Industrial Provident Societies Act 1986.

The audit of a housing association will be governed by statute and the particular rules of the association as set down in its constitution. The Companies Act requires that the accounts must reflect a true and fair view of the state of the finances of the association and the auditor is charged with the duty of verifying that view in the audit opinion. The Industrial and Provident Societies Act requires the auditor to check that an association has kept proper books of account relating to its transactions and its assets and liabilities. The Friendly and Industrial Provident Societies Act requires the auditor to check that proper books of account have been kept, financial statements are in agreement with those books and that there is sound internal control.

The Auditing Practices Committee issued an auditing guideline on Housing Associations in 1984 and this was embodied in a Housing Corporation Circular 45/89, *Code of Housing Association Audit Practice*. Broadly it defined the auditors' responsibilities as follows:

1. To undertake all audits in accordance with the appropriate APC standards and guidelines.
2. To report significant weaknesses in accounting and internal control in a management letter as required by the Housing Corporation.
3. To issue an audit report on the association's accounts in accordance with the Companies Act requirements.

Auditors must be members of approved professional accountancy bodies under the terms of the Companies Acts, and the Housing Corporation recommends that auditors should be changed around every seven years.

Areas for audit attention

The guideline identifies key audit areas requiring special consideration as:

- rents;
- service charges, water rates and council tax;
- repairs;
- grants;
- housing land;
- interest on land accrued;
- prohibited payments;
- donations and fund-raising;
- stocks and work in progress;
- mortgages receivable; and
- borrowing limits.

Auditing procedures

In planning the audit, auditors must take account of the auditing guideline,

Planning, controlling, and recording and additionally take the following into account:

- legislation affecting housing associations;
- the Recommended Form of Accounts;
- new Orders made by the Secretary of State under the 1980 Housing Act;
- circulars issued by the Department of the Environment and the Housing Corporation;
- changes affecting registered housing associations as reported by the NFHA; and
- any monitoring reported by the Housing Corporation.

As far as reviews of internal controls are concerned the guideline advises auditors to pay particular attention in smaller associations to poor segregation of duties. The guideline also warns auditors to be aware that the Housing Corporation may expect associations to require management letters from auditors and may expect such letters to be made available to itself.

CHAPTER 22
Nationalised and privatised industries

The nationalised industry sector is now a much less significant factor in the UK economy since the Conservative Government embarked upon a programme of privatisation which has yielded more than £33bn since 1979. The Conservative philosophy of 'rolling back the frontiers of the state' is founded on four principal assumptions. It argues that privatised industries will be more efficient once subjected to the rigours of the market place: competition will attract better management, streamline operations and produce a more customer-responsive organisation. Secondly, the sale of state owned assets will generate cash for other government purposes (debt reduction, capital investment or tax relief) though this benefit is a one-off gain. Thirdly, privatised industries will be able to develop clearer objectives which are disciplined by the markets and their shareholders rather than the changing policies of politicians. Lastly, privatisation offers the prospect of attracting private funds to promote investment whilst at the same time reducing the need for public sector borrowing.

In 1984/85 there were 22 nationalised industries with external financing limits (EFLs) of £3.9 billion. By 1992/93 these were reduced to eight with an EFL of just £1.5 billion. The major industries still in public ownership comprise British Coal, British Rail, London Regional Transport, the Post Office, Girobank, the water industry in Scotland, British Waterways Board and the Northern Ireland Electricity Board. It is doubtful whether all these will remain in public ownership by the end of the decade. Privatisation proposals for British Rail have already been presented to Parliament. Northern Ireland Electricity will follow its British mainland counterparts into the private sector and British Coal is struggling to find a market for its coal since electricity privatisation and the emergence of combined cycle gas generating plants in the energy market.

The external audit arrangements for the privatised industries are dictated by the statutory provisions within the individual privatisation acts. All of them are now subject to the general provisions of the Companies Act 1985.

A significant proportion of them are amongst the top 100 UK listed companies and the stewardship of their public service activities is no less subject to public scrutiny than in their former existence as publicly owned bodies.

Competition has not been as evident as many consumers would wish. British Gas and British Telecom in particular still hold near monopoly positions and the Government has adopted the American example of providing a regulator for many privatised industries (such as OFTEL for the telecommunications industry and OFWAT for the water industry) to act as the consumer go-between on pricing, profits, encouraging competition and safeguarding environmental interests.

Whilst market discipline will go some way in securing the intended improvements in productivity and service, the role of the regulators (for gas, telecom, water and electricity) will create shareholder uncertainty through their influence in capping price levels and the encouragement (sometimes with bias) of new competitors. Moreover there is the constant threat of examination by the Monopolies and Mergers Commission whilst Select Committee reviews (such as the 1992 coal pit closure proposals) may have consequential impact on the business plans of the privatised industries (in this case, the electricity companies which represent the largest market for coal).

The various statutes provide for the appointment usually annually, by the appropriate Minister or Secretary of State, of auditors who are members of one of the specified accountancy bodies under the terms of the Companies Act.

Scope of work

The statutory audit provision for nationalised and privatised industries tends to be short and does not set out the detailed responsibilities of the auditors as in the case, for example, of external auditors for local government. These responsibilities should not be regarded as being less onerous than those of other external auditors in the public sector and company auditors. For example, one would expect them to include references to the following:

1. Opinion on the 'true and fair' view of the accounts.
2. Compliance with ministerial direction on the form or substance of the accounts.
3. Non receipt of all information and explanations necessary for the audit.

In practice, too, the appropriate government department supplements the statutes by letters of appointment setting out in more detail the basis on which the external auditor is expected to operate. For example, the auditor is expected to verify:

• Whether the annual statement of accounts in the auditor's opinion gives a true and fair view of the state of affairs of the industry at the end of the accounting year and of the profit and loss of the year.

- Whether the accounts give the information required under the appropriate Act.
- Whether the Secretary of State is satisfied that the industry has complied with any notification or directions about the form and substance of the accounts.
- Whether proper accounts and other records have been kept by the industry.
- Whether the industry's annual statement of accounts is in agreement with the books of account and other records.
- Whether the Secretary of State has received all the information and explanations which are deemed necessary for the purposes of the audit.

In addition to expressing a professional opinion on the annual accounts, the auditor is normally expected to report on:

- Any material items of account which are not in accordance with the provisions of the appropriate legislation.
- Any inadequacies in the industry's procedure for ensuring compliance with government controls on external finance and financial targets.
- Any significant losses due to misconduct and fraud and other irregularities, which either were disclosed in the course of the audit or have been discovered by the industry's management during the accounting year.
- Any occasion revealed by the audit when, in their opinion, the industry's board or officers have fallen short of the high standards of financial integrity expected of those responsible for the management of public assets.
- Any significant weaknesses in the industry's administrative arrangements or systems, revealed during the course of the audit or by tests carried out, which in the auditor's opinion may result in losses, wasteful or extravagant expenditure or failure of the authority to conduct its financial affairs.
- Any other matter which the auditor considers requires a report.

The appropriate government department expects the audit to be performed in accordance with approved APB auditing standards and the work programmes should be designed accordingly. In particular, the audit work should include the following:

- Tests designed to satisfy the auditor as to the provisions made by the industry to minimise the risk of loss due to fraud, serious defalcation or other major irregularities.
- Appropriate tests on arrangements with agencies to enable an audit opinion to be unrestricted as to scope.

The big omission in relation to the external audit of most of these industries is any obligation upon the statutory audit in respect of value for money reviews. However, the National Audit Office audits the regulatory offices and can undertake VFM studies of them and hence the regulatory process.

Reporting

The reports and accounts of the nationalised and privatised industries are audited to give a clear and independent statement of whether they present a true and fair view of the financial position of the industry. The auditors are appointed either by the Secretaries of State of the sponsoring departments in respect of nationalised industries or by the respective boards of directors in respect of privatised industries. However, the conduct of the audit should conform to audit standards, guidelines and best practice, and qualifications of accounts, where necessary, stated from the standpoint of audit independence and professional judgement. An important fact is that in addition to the usual basis on which an opinion must be given, the auditors have to certify that legislation and ministerial directives given to an industry have been followed in preparing the accounts. Within this general context, there are two aspects of audit worthy of consideration, namely audit committees and the impact of audit qualifications.

Audit committees

Several of the nationalised industries and all the major privatised companies (British Telecom, British Gas, British Airways, British Steel, the Electricity Generators and the twelve regional electricity companies in England and Wales) operate with audit committees comprising non-executive directors. The committees, usually comprising the board's own members, handle the appointment of the statutory auditors and receive their reports and examine efficiency measures and performance in addition to the customary role of examining the accounts. The committees usually review the work and findings of the industry's own internal auditors and can commission reports on operational audits to procure greater efficiency in resource usage. These committees help to ensure action is taken to implement the recommendations of any review body, whether external or internal.

Audit qualifications for nationalised industries

The significance of partial qualifications to audit opinions on the accounts needs to be examined. In some instances, these have occurred in consecutive years. In the private sector this may have had particular consequences: for example, a fall in share prices or weakened ability to secure future finance. In the nationalised industries where this has occurred, any consequences which have arisen are not clear. This simply illustrates the special setting in which the nationalised industries operate, being removed from market forces but managed at arm's length, and in effect having only one shareholder, the Government. Public information on remedial action to overcome the cause of the qualifications has, therefore, to be centred on extensions in public debate about their significance. This could be achieved through ministerial statements, reviews by the relevant select committee, or more extensive coverage in the subsequent annual reports and accounts of the industry.

APB auditing guideline:
Guidance for Internal Auditors

This guideline provides advice to internal auditors about the main issues and procedures which they need to consider as part of their work. It should also be of benefit to organisations considering establishing an internal audit function.

The guideline is written in the context of internal audit work in both the commercial and public sectors. It should be read in conjunction with the Explanatory Forward to Auditing Standards and Guidelines and the Auditing Guidelines "Reliance on internal audit" and "The auditor's responsibility in relation to fraud, other irregularities and errors." Internal auditors may also find it helpful to refer to the Audit Brief "Value for money audit" issued by the Auditing Practices Committee [now Board] of CCAB Ltd (June 1990).

Internal auditors should also have regard to the ethical statements issued by the accountancy bodies and also to any requirements regarding internal audit set out in relevant statutes or regulations.

Objectives and scope of internal audit

1. Internal audit is an independent appraisal function established by the management of an organisation for the review of the internal control system as a service to the organisation. It objectively examines, evaluates and reports on the adequacy of internal control as a contribution to the proper, economic, efficient and effective use of resources.

2. The essentials for effective internal auditing are:

   (a) independence
       The internal auditor should have the independence in terms of organisational status and personal objectivity which permits the proper performance of his duties.

   (b) staffing and training
       The internal audit unit should be appropriately staffed in terms of

numbers, grades, qualifications and experience, having regard to its responsibilities and objectives. The internal auditor should be properly trained to fulfil all his responsibilities.

(c) relationships

The internal auditor should seek to foster constructive working relationships and mutual understanding with management, with external auditors, with any other review agencies and, where one exists, with the audit committee.

(d) due care

The internal auditor should exercise due care in fulfilling his responsibilities.

(e) planning, controlling and recording

The internal auditor should adequately plan, control and record his work.

(f) evaluation of the internal control system

The internal auditor should identify and evaluate the organisation's internal control system as a basis for reporting upon its adequacy and effectiveness.

(g) evidence

The internal auditor should obtain sufficient, relevant and reliable evidence on which to base reasonable conclusions and recommendations.

(h) reporting and follow-up

The internal auditor should ensure that findings, conclusions and recommendations arising from each internal audit assignment are communicated promptly to the appropriate level of management and he should actively seek a response. He should ensure that arrangements are made to follow up audit recommendations to monitor what action has been taken on them.

3. The terms of reference for the internal audit function should be formally confirmed by the organisation and should have proper regard to the contents of this guideline; demonstrable independence of the function is crucial to its effectiveness.

4. For certain public sector organisations the need for an internal auditing function is prescribed by statute and this provides a basis for defining specific standards and guidance for the practice of internal auditing in those organisations. The Government internal audit manual and the National Health Service internal audit manual are examples of internal auditing standards and guidance prescribed for specific organisations.

5. To achieve full effectiveness the scope of the internal audit function should provide an unrestricted range of coverage of the organisation's operations, and the internal auditor should have sufficient authority to allow him access to such records, assets and personnel as are necessary for proper fulfilment of his responsibilities.

6. It is a management responsibility to determine the extent of internal control in the organisation's systems which should not depend on internal audit as a substitute for effective controls. Internal audit, as a service to the organisation, contributes to internal control by examining, evaluating and reporting to management on its adequacy and effectiveness. Internal audit activity may lead to the strengthening of internal control as a result of management response.

7. One of the objectives of internal auditing is to assist management in the pursuit of value for money. It is achieved through economic, efficient and effective use of resources.

8. It is a management responsibility to maintain the internal control system and to ensure that the organisation's resources are properly applied in the manner and on the activities intended. This includes responsibility for the prevention and detection of fraud and other illegal acts.

9. The internal auditor should have regard to the possibility of such malpractice and should seek to identify serious defects in internal control which might permit the occurrence of such an event.

10. An internal auditor who discovers evidence of, or suspects, malpractice should report firm evidence, or reasonable suspicions, to the appropriate level of management. It is a management responsibility to determine what further action to take.

Independence

11. Independence is achieved through the organisational status of internal audit and the objectivity of internal auditors.

Organisational status

12. The status of internal audit should enable it to function effectively. The support of management is essential. Internal audit should be involved in the determination of its own priorities, in consultation with management. Accordingly the head of internal audit should have direct access to, and freedom to report to, all senior management including the chief executive, board of directors and, where one exists, the audit committee.

Objectivity of the internal auditor

13. Each internal auditor should have an objective attitude of mind and be in a sufficiently independent position to be able to exercise judgement, express opinions and present recommendations with impartiality.

   (a) The internal auditor, notwithstanding his employment by the organisation, should be free from any conflict of interest arising either from professional or personal relationships or from pecuniary or other interests in an organisation or activity which is subject to audit.

(b) The internal auditor should be free from undue influences which either restrict or modify the scope of conduct of his work or over-rule or significantly affect judgement as to the content of the internal audit report.

(c) The internal auditor should not allow his objectivity to be impaired when auditing an activity for which he has had authority or responsibility.

(d) An internal auditor should be consulted about significant proposed changes in the internal control system and the implementation of new systems and make recommendations on the standards of control to be applied. This need not prejudice that auditor's objectivity in reviewing those systems subsequently.

(e) An internal auditor should not normally undertake non-audit duties but where he does so, exceptionally, he should ensure that management understands that he is not then functioning as an internal auditor.

14. Where any of the situations referred to in paragraphs 13(a) to (c) arise, this should be clearly declared by the internal auditor so that consideration can be given to the need for alternative arrangements for the audit assignment.

Staffing and training

15. The effectiveness of internal audit depends substantially on the quality, training and experience of its staff. The aim should be to appoint staff with the appropriate background, personal qualities and potential. Thereafter, steps should be taken to provide the necessary experience, training and continuing professional education.

Staffing

16. The internal audit unit should be managed by a head of internal audit who should be suitably qualified and should possess wide experience of internal audit and of its management. He should plan, direct, control and motivate the resources available to ensure that the responsibilities of the internal audit unit are met.

17. The full range of duties may require internal audit staff to be drawn from a variety of disciplines. The effectiveness of internal audit may be enhanced by the use of specialist staff, particularly in the internal audit of activities of a technical nature.

18. The internal audit unit should employ staff with varying types and levels of skills, qualifications and experience in order to satisfy the requirements of each internal audit task.
19. The head of internal audit should participate in the recruitment and selection of his staff. New entrants to internal audit work should have time to familiarise themselves with the activities of their internal audit unit and the organisation, and to demonstrate their suitability for audit work.

Training

20. The organisation has a responsibility to ensure that the internal auditor receives the training necessary for the performance of the full range of duties.
21. Training should be tailored to the needs of the individual. It should include both the theoretical knowledge and its practical application under the supervision of suitably competent and experienced internal auditors. Account should be taken of:

    (a) internal audit objectives and priorities;
    (b) the type of internal audit work;
    (c) previous training, experience and qualifications; and
    (d) personal development in the light of the needs of the organisation and the internal audit unit.

22. Training should be a planned and continuing process at all levels and should cover:

    (a) basic training – providing the knowledge of basic auditing principles and practices which all internal auditors should possess;
    (b) development training – in general audit skills and techniques and inter-personal skills, to improve the effectiveness of those currently employed in internal audit; and
    (c) specialised training – for those responsible for the internal audit activities which require special skills or knowledge.

23. Other forms of staff development should be considered according to particular needs. These may include periods of attachment to other parts of the organisation or secondment to other organisations.
24. The internal auditor should keep abreast of current developments, improvements, new techniques and practices in auditing.
25. The internal auditor should maintain technical competence through professional development which may include:

    (a) private reading and study; and
    (b) participation in professional activities such as attending meetings, courses and conferences, lecturing, writing articles and papers and contributions to research groups.

26. The head of internal audit should co-ordinate, and keep under review, the training requirements of internal auditors. He should be responsible for preparing training profiles which identify the training requirements for different grades of internal auditor, and should maintain personal training records for each individual. In large organisations this may be performed by a designated training officer.

Relationships

27. In order that the internal auditor may properly perform all his tasks, it is necessary for all those with whom he has contact to have confidence in him. Constructive working relationships make it more likely that internal audit work will be accepted and acted upon, but the internal auditor should not allow his objectivity to be impaired.

Organisational relationships

28. The head of internal audit should prepare the internal audit plan in consultation with senior management. The internal auditor should arrange the timing of internal audit assignments with the management concerned, except on those rare occasions where an unannounced visit is a necessary part of the audit approach. Consultation can lead to the identification of areas of concern or of other interest to management.
29. Matters which arise in the course of the audit are confidential and discussion should be restricted to management directly responsible for the area being audited unless they have given express agreement to broaden the discussion.
30. Discussions with management are necessary when preparing the audit report. This is an essential feature of the good relationship between the auditor and the management.

Relationships with external audit

31. The relationship between internal and external audit needs to take account of their differing roles and responsibilities. Internal audit is an independent appraisal function within the organisation and internal auditors are direct employees. The external auditor usually has a statutory responsibility to express an independent opinion on the financial statements and stewardship of the organisation.
32. The aim should be to achieve mutual recognition and respect, leading to a joint improvement in performance and the avoidance of unnecessary over-lapping of work. It should be possible for the external and internal auditors to rely on each other's work, subject to limits determined by

their different responsibilities, respective strengths and special abilities. Consultations should be held and consideration given to whether any work of either auditor is adequate for the purpose of the other. The internal auditor does not automatically have a right of access to the records of the external auditor. However, the relationship between the internal and external auditor will usually be such that the external auditor will be able to allow access to the necessary records.

33. Since internal audit evaluates an organisation's internal control system the external auditor may need to be satisfied that the internal audit function is being planned and performed effectively. This review needs to be seen by both parties as a necessary part of the working relationship (see the Auditing Guideline 'Reliance on internal audit').

34. Regular meetings should be held between internal and external auditors at which joint audit planning, priorities, scope and audit findings are discussed and information exchanged. The benefits of joint training programmes and joint audit work should also be considered.

Review agencies and specialists

35. Certain information obtained during an internal audit assignment may assist a review agency, such as management services or consultants, which is seeking to secure improvements in the organisation's performance. Management's formal approval should be obtained before releasing any audit report or other information to a review agency.

36. The internal auditor should establish a regular dialogue with review agencies and obtain their reports for information, for review and for comment where proposals may affect internal control arrangements.

37. Where it is necessary for the internal auditor to have contact with other specialists the same basic principles about information apply as in the case of review agencies.

Due care

38. The internal auditor cannot be expected to give total assurance that control weaknesses or irregularities do not exist.

39. In order to demonstrate that due care has been exercised the internal auditor should be able to show that his work has been performed in a way which is consistent with this guideline.

40. The internal auditor should possess a thorough knowledge of the aims of the organisation and the internal control system. He should also be aware of the relevant law and the requirements of relevant professional and regulatory bodies.

Ethical standards

41. The ethical statements issued by the accountancy bodies are relevant to the work of internal auditors.
42. The internal auditor must be impartial in discharging all responsibilities; bias, prejudice or undue influence must not be allowed to limit or override objectivity. At all times, the integrity and conduct of each internal auditor must be above reproach. He should not place himself in a position where responsibilities and private interests conflict and any personal interest should be declared. Gifts or other rewards should not be accepted.
43. The internal auditor should not improperly disclose any information obtained during the course of his work.

Quality of internal audit performance

44. The head of internal audit should promote and maintain adequate quality standards in the internal audit unit. He should establish methods of evaluating the work of his staff to ensure that the internal audit unit fulfils its responsibilities and has proper regard to this guideline.

Planning, controlling and recording

45. Internal Audit work should be planned, controlled and recorded in order to determine priorities, establish and achieve objectives and ensure the effective and efficient use of audit resources.

Planning

46. The main purposes of internal audit planning are

   (a) to determine priorities and to establish the most cost-effective means of achieving audit objectives.
   (b) to assist in the direction and control of audit work.
   (c) to help ensure that attention is devoted to critical aspects of audit work, and
   (d) to help ensure that work is completed in accordance with pre-determined targets.

47. The stages of internal audit planning are:

   (a) to identify the objectives of the organisation.
   (b) to define internal audit objectives.
   (c) to take account of all relevant changes in legislation and other external factors.

(d) to obtain a comprehensive understanding of the organisation's systems, structure and operations.

(e) to identify, evaluate and rank risks to which the organisation is exposed.

(f) to take account of changes in structures or major systems in the organisation.

(g) to take account of known strengths and weaknesses in the internal control system.

(h) to take account of management concerns and expectations.

(i) to identify audit areas by service, functions and major systems.

(j) to determine the type of audit e.g. systems, verification or value for money.

(k) to take account of the plans of external audit and other review agencies.

(l) to assess staff resources required and match with resources available.

48. The internal auditor should prepare strategic, periodic and operational workplans.

49. This will usually cover a period of two to five years during which time all major systems and areas of activity will be audited. It will set out the audit objectives, audit areas, type of activity, frequency of audit and an assessment of resources to be applied.

50. This will typically cover a financial or calendar year, translates the strategic plan into a schedule of audit assignments to be carried out in the ensuing period. It will define the purpose and duration of each audit assignment and allocate staff and other resources, accordingly and should be formally approved by management.

51. These should be prepared for each audit assignment as it is arranged, covering:-

(a) objectives and scope of the audit;

(b) time budget and staff allocation; and

(c) methods, procedure and reporting arrangements, including supervision and allocation of responsibilities.

52. All internal audit plans should be sufficiently flexible to respond to changing priorities.

Controlling

53. Control of the internal audit unit and of individual assignments is needed to ensure that internal audit objectives are achieved and work is performed effectively. The most important elements of control are the direction and supervision of the internal audit staff and review of their work. This will be assisted by an established audit approach and standard documentation.

The degree of control and supervision required depends on the complexity of assignments and the experience and proficiency of the internal audit staff.

54. The Head of Internal Audit should establish arrangements:-

    (a) to allocate internal audit assignments according to the level of and proficiency of internal audit staff.
    (b) to ensure that internal auditors clearly understand the responsibilities and internal audit objectives.
    (c) to communicate the scope of the work to be performed and agree the programme of work with each internal auditor.
    (d) to provide and document evidence of adequate supervision, review and guidance during the internal audit assignment.
    (e) to ensure that adequate working papers are being prepared to support internal audit findings and conclusions.
    (f) to ensure that internal audit's performance is in accordance with the internal audit plan or that any significant variations have been explained.

55. The Head of Internal Audit should establish arrangements to evaluate the performance of the internal audit unit. An annual report may also be prepared to management on the activities of the internal audit unit in which an assessment is given of how effectively the objectives of the function have been met.

Recording

56. Internal audit work should be properly recorded because:

    (a) the head of internal audit needs to be able to ensure that work delegated to staff has been properly performed. This can generally be done only by reference to detailed working papers prepared by the internal audit staff who performed the work.
    (b) working papers provide for future reference, evidence of work performed, details of problems encountered and conclusions drawn; and
    (c) the preparation of working papers encourages each internal auditor to adopt a methodical approach to work.

57. The Head of Internal Audit should specify the required standard of internal audit documentation and working papers and ensure that those standards are maintained.

58. Internal audit working papers should always be sufficiently complete and detailed to enable an experienced internal auditor, with no previous connection with the internal audit assignment subsequently to ascertain from them what work was performed and to support the conclusions

reached. Working papers should be prepared as the internal audit assignment proceeds so that critical details are not omitted and problems not overlooked. These should be reviewed by internal audit management.

Evaluation of the internal control system

59. Controls ensure that processes act to meet the system's objectives.
60. The main objectives of the internal control system are:

    (a) to ensure adherence to management policies and directives in order to achieve the organisation's objectives;
    (b) to safeguard assets;
    (c) to secure the relevance, reliability and integrity of information, so ensuring as far as possible the completeness and accuracy of records; and
    (d) to ensure compliance with statutory requirements.

61. When evaluating internal control systems the internal auditor should consider the effect which all the controls have on each other and on related systems.
62. As part of the planning process the internal auditor should identify the whole range of systems within the organisation. For those systems to be examined, the internal auditor should establish appropriate criteria to determine whether the controls are adequate and assist in achieving the objectives of the system. The stages of a systems audit would normally be:

    (a) To identify the systems parameters;
    (b) To determine the control objectives;
    (c) To identify expected controls to meet control objectives;
    (d) To review the system against expected controls;
    (e) To appraise the controls designed into the system against control objectives;
    (f) To test the actual controls for effectiveness against control objectives;
    (g) To test the operation of controls in practice;
    (h) To give an opinion based on audit objectives as to whether the system provides an adequate basis for effective control and whether it is properly operated in practice.

Evidence

63. Internal audit evidence is information obtained by an internal auditor which enables conclusions to be formed on which recommendations can be based.

64. The internal auditor should determine what evidence will be necessary by exercising judgement in the light of the objectives of the internal audit assignment. This judgement will be influenced by the scope of the assignment, the significance of the matters under review, the relevance and the reliability of available evidence and the cost and time involved in obtaining it.
65. The collection and assessment of internal audit evidence should be recorded and reviewed to provide reasonable assurance that conclusions are soundly based and internal audit objectives achieved.

Sufficiency

66. An internal auditor should obtain the evidence considered necessary for the achievement of the internal audit assignment objectives. This is influenced by, for instance:

   (a) the level of assurance required;
   (b) the objectives and scope of the internal audit assignment;
   (c) the scale of activity under review and the degree of risk involved;
   (d) the cost and time involved in obtaining evidence; and
   (e) the reliability of the evidence.

Relevance

67. The relevance of the internal audit evidence should be considered in relation to the objectives of the internal audit assignment.

Reliability

68. Reliable evidence can be achieved through the use of the appropriate internal audit techniques which should normally be selected in advance, but which may be expanded or altered as necessary during the internal audit assignment.
69. In order to place reliance on evidence an internal auditor should be satisfied with its nature, extent, adequacy, consistency and relevance to the internal audit assignment and with the methods governing its collection.

Reporting and follow-up

70. The primary purpose of internal audit reports are to provide management with an opinion on the adequacy of the internal control system, and to inform management of significant audit findings, conclusions and recommendations. The aim of every internal audit report should be:

(a) to prompt management action to implement recommendations for change leading to improvement in performance and control; and

(b) to provide a formal record of points arising from the internal audit assignment and, where appropriate, of agreements reached with management.

71. Reporting arrangements, including the format and distribution of internal audit reports, should be agreed with management. The Head of Internal Audit should ensure that reports are sent to managers who have a direct responsibility for the unit or function being audited and who have the authority to take action on the internal audit recommendations. Internal audit reports are confidential documents and their distribution should be restricted to those managers who need to know, to the Audit Committee and to the external auditor.

72. While the internal auditor may clear minor matters which do not indicate a consistent or systematic weakness with members of staff directly involved, matters of consequence should be reported formally in writing to management.

73. The internal auditor should produce clear, constructive and concise written reports based on sufficient, relevant and reliable evidence, which should:

(a) state the scope, purpose, extent and conclusions of the internal audit assignment;

(b) make recommendations which are appropriate and relevant, and which flow from the conclusions; and

(c) acknowledge the action taken, or proposed, by management.

74. The internal auditor should make an interim report, orally or in writing, where it is necessary to alert management to the need to take immediate action to correct a serious weakness in performance or control, or where there are reasonable grounds for suspicion of malpractice. Considerations should also be given to interim reporting where there is a significant change in scope of the internal audit assignment or where it is desirable to inform management of progress. Interim reporting does not diminish or eliminate the need for final reporting.

75. The internal auditor should normally meet with management to discuss audit findings at the completion of fieldwork for each internal audit assignment and the formal written report should be presented to management as soon as possible thereafter.

76. Before issuing the final report, the internal auditor should normally discuss the contents with the appropriate levels of management, and may submit a draft report to them, for confirmation of factual accuracy.

77. If the internal auditor and management disagree about the relevance of the factual content of the draft audit report, the internal auditor should consider whether reference should be made to this in the final report.

78. It is management's responsibility to ensure that proper consideration is given to internal audit reports. The internal auditor should ensure that appropriate arrangements are made to determine whether action has been taken on internal audit recommendations or that management has understood and assumed the risk of not taking action.

Examples of basic audit programmes

Basic audit programme

WAGES/SALARIES

1. *Objectives*

1.1 To appraise the approved procedures and see that they are followed, that the payments made are correct and are in accordance with national/local agreements, that the records maintained are accurate and adequate, and proper security is exercised over collection, make-up, custody and pay-out of cash or cheques.

2. *Area of audit*

2.1 Commences where a wage/salary becomes due.
2.2 Finishes with the payment to the employee and posting in the financial records.

3. *Basic programme*

CONTROL

Review the system of control in order to verify the following:

3.1 That adequate and up-to-date records, covering all staff gradings and other entitlements, are maintained.
3.2 That there is an adequate system for the control of starters and leavers.
3.3 That adequate procedures exist for the authorisation of amendments to the record for new starters, leavers, salary changes, etc., and that these are properly actioned.
3.4 That daily, weekly and monthly time records (where appropriate) are properly certified.
3.5 That any additional payments (overtime, bonus, sick pay, etc.) are correctly calculated and supported by the correct documentation and are correctly authorised.
3.6 That control is exercised over input documentation in order to prevent duplication, loss or incorrect submission.
3.7 That there is control over all types of deduction and that these are paid, in due course, to the correct authority.
3.8 That gross and net pay totals are controlled in the financial records and

that pay-out procedures are clearly defined regarding security, identification and receipting.

Verify, by sample, or physically where necessary, the following:

3.9 The employment authorities and rates of pay (including additional payments, such as allowances).

3.10 The calculation of hours as booked on time records (if appropriate).

3.11 The amendments to rates of pay.

3.12 The calculation of gross pay.

3.13 That the deductions/refunds (statutory and voluntary) are properly authorised and correctly made.

3.14 That statutory and voluntary deductions are paid to the appropriate payees at the prescribed intervals.

3.15 The calculation of net pay.

3.16 The summarising of gross pay, deductions and net pay and the posting of totals to the financial records.

3.17 That the total wage/salary cheque(s) are reconciled with the payroll.

3.18 That procedures are adequate for payment by the following means:

3.18.1 BACS (Bankers Automated Clearing Services).

3.18.2 Cheque.

3.18.3 Cash.

3.18.4 Other – (please specify).

3.19 That security and other procedures, including identification, are adequate in respect of the following:

3.19.1 The collection and custody of bulk cash.

3.19.2 The make-up of net wages/salaries.

3.19.3 The pay-out of net wages/salaries.

3.19.4 The control and accounting for unclaimed wages/salaries.

3.20 That each employee has a national insurance record.

4. *Main areas of internal control*

4.1 There should be clearly defined details of duties and responsibilities for all personnel involved in payroll procedures.

4.2 There should be a proper authorisation for the engagement and discharge of employees.

4.3 There should be an adequate record covering all staff gradings and other entitlements and amendments, only made on the authorisation of an approved officer.

4.4 There should be a properly authorised notification for any payments made in addition to basic salary.

4.5 Voluntary deductions should only be made with the proper authority.

4.6 Adequate control accounts should be maintained for all deductions, and clearance of these is the responsibility of a senior officer.

4.7 There should be approval of the payroll by a responsible officer.

4.8 Wherever possible, salary payments should be by direct transfer.

4.9 The cheque(s) drawn to meet salary payments must equal the net payroll total.

4.10 Unclaimed wages/salary should be adequately controlled.

Basic audit programme

PAYROLL

Total number of staff on payroll	Payroll group or department ......
Authorised establishment	Code reference
Provision in estimates – current year	Week/month ended
Actual expenditure to date	Total basic pay
12 months equivalent	Total overtime

No.	Individual probe	(1) Name: Ref:	(2) Name: Ref:	(3) Name: Ref:	(4) Name: Ref:	(5) Name: Ref:	(6) Name: Ref:	(7) Name: Ref:	(8) Name: Ref:	(9) Name: Ref:	(10) Name: Ref:
	Appointment and history records										
1.	Verify that post is within approved establishment										
2.	Ensure that post and grading for rate of pay were properly authorised.										
3.	Verify that recognised appointment procedure was followed.										
4.	If employee holds a second appointment, apply probes 1, 2 & 3 and include in following probes.										
5.	Ensure that current data held on magnetic tape, as evidenced by print-out, has been checked and agreed with current entries on the payroll record card.										
6.	Ensure that a permanent record is kept of the employee's service sufficient to cover the data required for possible future entry to superannuation scheme and possible payment due under redundancy payments scheme.										

	(1)	(2)	(3)	(4)	(5)	(6)	(7)	(8)	(9)	(10)

Calculation of gross pay

7. Verify correctness of grade.
8. Verify that current rate of pay is correct and the basic weekly/monthly amount is correctly calculated.
9. Verify that all additional payments have been properly authorised and correctly calculated.
10. Ensure that a satisfactory record of overtime worked is maintained within the department.
11. If payment under review includes overtime, state total amount paid during last three months.
12. Ensure that satisfactory time records or attendance records are maintained.

Deductions and net pay

13. Verify that *all* deductions due to be made have actually been made and ensure they are correctly assessed and calculated.
    (*a*) Superannuation
    (*b*) National Insurance
    (*c*) PAYE
    (*d*) Union fees
    (*e*) Housing advance
    (*f*) Car loan

Subsidiary Records

14. Ensure that all advances, grants, loans, etc., which are recoverable or may be recoverable on leaving have been properly recorded on the payroll record card and magnetic tape store (see print-out).

		(1)	(2)	(3)	(4)	(5)	(6)	(7)	(8)	(9)	(10)
15.	Ensure that the superannuation data given on payroll record card agrees with the superannuation personnel record and this agrees with the personal file.										
16.	Verify that the total of superannuation contributions for the last financial year as shown by the last payroll for that period agrees with the total amount shown on the computer print-out of contributions.										
17.	Verify that the total tax deductions and National Insurance contributions for the last ended year as shown on the final payroll agree with the figures shown on P35 computer substitute return.										

Sickness

		(1)	(2)	(3)	(4)	(5)	(6)	(7)	(8)	(9)	(10)
18.	Ensure that a proper record is kept of all absences through sickness.										
19.	Verify that any sickness payments made during the past six months have been correctly calculated and the payments correctly recorded.										

Payment of wages/salary

		(1)	(2)	(3)	(4)	(5)	(6)	(7)	(8)	(9)	(10)
20.	If paid in cash: (a) Ensure that the payroll has been signed with the employee's normal signature and that the paying officer has properly certified the payroll.										

	(1)	(2)	(3)	(4)	(5)	(6)	(7)	(8)	(9)	(10)
(*b*) Ensure that a satisfactory record is kept of unclaimed wages and the disposal thereof.										
(*c*) Ensure that the security for retention of unclaimed wages is good and that if they are not claimed within three weeks that they are repaid to bank.										
(*d*) Ensure that the security arrangements for the custody of cash drawn from the bank and the make-up of pay are satisfactory.										
21. If paid by cheque, verify that the paid cheque has been examined and found to be in order.										
22. If pay is forwarded to a home address, ensure that there is a satisfactory reason for this and that the name and address appear in the Register of Electors.										
23. If paid by cheque, ensure that if there were any special instructions with regard to despatch there were satisfactory reasons for such instructions.										
24. If paid by bank credit, verify that the amount has been agreed with the print-out of the magnetic tape and that the total of the print-out agrees with the debit in the bank statement.										
Leave										
25. Ensure that a proper record of all absences on annual										

	(1)	(2)	(3)	(4)	(5)	(6)	(7)	(8)	(9)	(10)
	leave or special leave is maintained.									
26.	Ensure that the amount of leave taken as recorded during the last year was within the official entitlement or authorised if special leave.									

Training

27.	Ensure that all absences on post-entry training courses during the last twelve months have been properly recorded on the official training record for purposes of claiming grant (if applicable).									
28.	Ensure that all payments of fees, expenses or grants on training courses during the last twelve months have been properly recorded on the official training record.									

		ANSWER
29.	*Internal control* Ensure that the proper procedures were followed and the agreed internal check arrangements were fully documented and observed, i.e.,	
(*a*)	*Engaging employees* (*i*) Who engages employees? (*ii*) Are any employees engaged at the establishment where they will normally work? (*iii*) Are any persons engaged by the person who will be responsible for supervising them during their normal working day?	

ANSWER

(*iv*) Are there any special provisions operative for the engagement of temporary staff?

(*b*) *Time records (where appropriate)*
(*i*) What time-recording system is in operation?
(*ii*) Who completes the time sheet?
(*iii*) Who certifies the time sheet and what are his daily relations with the employee? Is this the same person who engages staff?
(*iv*) What independent check is made of the time sheet against the original time record?

(*c*) *Establishment control*
(*i*) What control exists to ensure that the approved establishment is adhered to?
(*ii*) Are there written authorities for the following:
new employees;
retirements, transfers, resignations, dismissals and changes;
gradings;
individual payroll deductions other than compulsory deductions?
Are these documents certified by persons so authorised?
Are specimen signatures of the authorisation held by salaries/wages section?

(*d*) Are appointment forms used?
If so, how are they controlled?
What control exists to show the salaries/wages section that an employee has been properly appointed?

(*e*) *Payment*
(*i*) Who hands out wage/salary packets/cheques/slips?
(*ii*) Is this the same person who also engages employees and/or certifies time sheets?

(f)	*Other comments*	

Payroll probe carried out by:

Audit assistant... Date............

Audit team leader .... Date............

Chief internal auditor.. Date............

Man-day allocation

Allocated	Taken	Reasons for variation

Basic audit programme

CREDITORS – INVOICE PAYMENTS

1. *Objectives*

   To ensure that the system and controls provide the following:

1.1 That all payments made are in respect of goods received and services rendered to the organisation and that these have been properly ordered.

2. *Area of audit*

2.1 Commences at the creditor's invoice.
2.2 Finishes at the cheque payments and postings to expenditure records.

3. *Basic programme*

   Review the system of control, in order to ensure the following:

3.1 That all goods and services received are adequately covered by official documentation.
3.2 That all invoices paid are authorised in accordance with policy and that adequate procedures exist for the control of payments where no official order is issued.
3.3 That adequate control exists for the raising of, amendments to, and the deletion of standing periodic payments.
3.4 That control exists over the allocation and usage of creditors' reference numbers.
3.5 That control exists for the reconciliation of expenditure totals – invoice batch totals and cheque list totals.
3.6 That adequate division of duties exists in order to obviate the inclusion of 'dummy invoices'.

INVOICE PAYMENT RECORDS

By sample, verify the following:

3.7 That invoice certification is in accordance with laid down procedures.
3.8 That invoices paid are supported by copy orders, goods received or return notes, or other approved form of official documentation.
3.9 That approved authorisation exists for raising and amending periodic payments.
3.10 That there is no undue delay in the payment of invoices and recovery of credits.
3.11 That cash settlement discounts are being taken where applicable.
3.12 That the cost coding of invoices is correct and agrees with expenditure records.
3.13 That cheque payment records agree with invoice batch control register totals and expenditure totals.

GENERAL

3.14 Examine records and procedures and verify that controls exist which cover payments made against documents raised internally.

3.15 Examine procedures for control over the usages and stocks of unused cheques.

3.16 Verify that adequate controls exist which cover special or quick payments made manually.

3.17 Examine the control over payments which are made against duplicate invoices and reasons for so doing.

4.   *Main areas of internal control*

4.1 There should be an adequate system of internal check with proper controls and division of duties.

4.2 Lists of approved signatories should be available covering all employees who have the authority to authorise payments.

4.3 Proper procedures should exist for control over the raising of, and amendments to, periodic payments.

4.4 There should be adequate and independent control over the usage and stocks of cheques, particularly where pre-signed cheques are used.

4.5 There should be a control register of creditors. Reference numbers and the issue and deletion of numbers should be strictly controlled.

4.6 There should be a periodic review of all unprocessed invoices.

4.7 A procedure for the cancellation of paid invoices should be in operation.

4.8 Adequate procedural checks should be carried out in all cases where payment is requested against duplicate/copy invoices.

4.9 There should be control procedures for the raising of cheques against pro-forma invoices/cheque requisitions which are raised internally.

Basic audit programme

CREDITORS

Payee	Batch No. .....
	Date of payment ......
Brief details of payment	Amount £
	Date of invoice ....

Provision in estimates	Formal agreement if any
Actual to date	Committee minute

(1) Individual probes (if a probe is not applicable then mark N/A in tick column)	(2) If answer as shown below tick here ▼	(3) If answer is not as in column (2) enter below with comments
Ordering		
1. Was an official order used?	Yes	
(*a*) If so, was it made out before purchase?	Yes	
(*b*) Do quantities and qualities agree with invoice?	Yes	
(*c*) Has the copy order been marked as 'passed for payment' with the date?	Yes	
(*d*) Is the person signing the order authorised to do so?	Yes	
2. Is authority to order restricted to specified officers? (Please supply brief details.)	Yes ──────►	
Are orders actually signed by these officers?	Yes	
3. Are order books adequately controlled?	Yes	
4. Are orders supported by requisition?	Yes	
5. What is the procedure for dealing with verbal orders/emergency orders/open orders, etc.? (Please give brief details.)	──────►	

(1) Individual probes (if a probe is not applicable then mark N/A in tick column)	(2) If answer as shown below tick here ▼	(3) If answer is not as in column (2) enter below with comments
Receiving		
6. (a) Did the person who signed 'goods received' in the certification actually receive and check the goods?	Yes	
(b) (i) If not, did he before initialling check with a delivery note or goods received note signed by the person receiving?	Yes	
(ii) If answer to last probe is 'yes', have you seen the delivery note and verified the identity of the person signing?	Yes	
7. If it is an item where delivery note would normally be sent, check the delivery note with the invoice.	Checked	
8. If it is a stock item then (a) check the entry in the records, and	Checked	
(b) verify present physical stock.	Checked	
9. If it is an inventory item then either (a) check entry in inventory and verify existence, or	Checked	
(b) note in appropriate file for physical checking on next visit.	Noted	
10. If the item should be entered in a goods received book, then check the entry.	Checked	
11. Is the person signing the 'goods received' certification or delivery note the same person who signed the official order (or who gave the order, if no official order)?	No	

(1) Individual probes (if a probe is not applicable then mark N/A in tick column)	(2) If answer as shown below tick here	(3) If answer is not as in column (2) enter below with comments
Certification and prices		
12. (a) Is the invoice arithmetically correct?	Yes	
(b) Were tenders or quotations obtained?	Yes	
If so, are prices in accordance therewith?	Yes	
(c) If quotations were obtained:		
(i) Was the lowest accepted	Yes	
(ii) If not, was an appropriate report made to the Committee?	Yes	
(d) If the cost of work was estimated, does the actual show an increase?	No	
(e) If the item purchased is an annual contract of any other department:		
(i) Is the price paid higher than the rate applicable to the other department?	No	
(ii) If the price is lower, has the other department been notified?		
(iii) At what prices do neighbouring organisations obtain similar goods?		
(f) (i) Is the coding allocation correct?	Yes	
(ii) Is the budget head overspent?	No	
(iii) If capital, has an entry been made in capital ledger?	Yes	
(g) Have all possible discounts and allowances been deducted?	Yes	
13. (a) Is there an approved list of certifying officers?	Yes	

(1) Individual probes (if a probe is not applicable then mark N/A in tick column)	(2) If answer as shown below tick here	(3) If answer is not as in column (2) enter below with comments
(*b*) Are invoices actually certified by these officers?	Yes	
(*c*) Is the certification by facsimile signature?	Yes	
If so, are the stamps in safe custody?	Yes	
14. Does the certifying officer		
(*a*) Order supplies?	No	
(*b*) Receive supplies?	No	
15. (*a*) Have all the appropriate certifications in the 'block' been completed?	Yes	
(*b*) Have the initials, etc., of persons certifying in the 'block' been identified?	Yes	
(*c*) Have the persons so identified the necessary authority to certify?	Yes	
(*d*) Has VAT been dealt with correctly?	Yes	
General		
16. (*a*) Is the invoice addressed to the organisation?	Yes	
(*b*) Is the invoice on the creditor's own bill-head?	Yes	
If not,		
(*i*) Are there any suspicious features revealed by examination of paid cheque?	No	
(*ii*) Does the name and address appear in the telephone directory *or*	Yes	
Register of Electors?	Yes	
(*iii*) Does question 11 apply?	No	
17. Is there a possibility of income being due to the organisation?	No	

(1) Individual probes (if a probe is not applicable then mark N/A in tick column)	(2) If answer as shown below tick here	(3) If answer is not as in column (2) enter below with comments
18. Is the quantity ordered (a) excessive having regard to requirements or existing stocks?	No	
(b) insufficient having regard to possible 'bulk purchase' savings?	No	
19. Is there sufficient description on the invoice to identify clearly the items purchased?	Yes	
20. Has this description been inserted by the supplier? (If not, by whom?)	Yes	
21. (a) Do the name and amount on the paid cheque agree with the details		
(i) on the invoice, and	Yes	
(ii) in the copy cash book?	Yes	
(b) Are there any suspicious or undesirable features with regard to the person to whom the cheque is made payable? (see question 16 (b).)	No	
22. Has there been any prolonged and undue delay in either the rendering of the invoice or passing the account for payment? If so, state reasons.	No	→
23. If the payment was made as an 'urgent payment' was this justified?	Yes	
24. If the item is a periodical payment, check the 'p.p.' entry for accuracy and watch duplicate payment possibility.	Checked	
25. Were there any specific instructions for handing the cheque to any person? If so, to whom and why?	No	→

(1) Individual probes (if a probe is not applicable then mark N/A in tick column)	(2) If answer as shown below tick here	(3) If answer is not as in column (2) enter below with comments
Procedures generally 26. Have standing orders and financial regulations been complied with?	Yes	
27. Any comments on internal control or procedures generally whether directly or indirectly concerned with the payment.		
Observations 28. In answering the questions enumerated in this questionnaire it may be necessary to ask supplementary questions to establish the full facts. Similarly, there may be significant information arising from this inquiry not specifically covered here, but nevertheless relevant. The facts should be recorded.		

Audit probe carried out by:

Audit assistant .... Date............

Audit team leader.. Date............

Chief internal auditor .... Date............

Basic audit programme

CASH COLLECTION

1. *Objectives*

1.1 To verify that the procedures for the security, collection, receipting and recording of all cash are adequate and in accordance with procedures.
1.2 To ensure that all cash collected is correctly banked without delay.
1.3 To ensure that the system is adequate, in order that the postings to the relevant accounts will be carried out correctly and promptly.

2. *Area of audit*

2.1 Commences at the receipt of cash at all types of collection points.
2.2 Finishes at the banking of the cash and posting to the accounting records, and the carrying out of a regular reconciliation of all bank accounts.

3. *Basic programme*

CONTROL

3.1 Review and test that the system provides for control of all types of receipts.
3.2 Verify that the system ensures the adequate recording of all monies received from all sources, including postal remittances.
3.3 Verify that the system means that collections are banked without delay on a daily basis.
3.4 Review the system of internal control and check that there is an adequate division of duties within the cash section.

RECEIPT CONTROL, CASH COLLECTION AND BANKING RECORDS

By sample, verify the following:

3.5 The control over stocks and issues and the daily usage of manual type receipts.
3.6 The control exercised over the usage of receipt books and machines.
3.7 That cash receipted from all types of sources has been correctly recorded.
3.8 That collections, including cheques, have been banked without delay.
3.9 That cashiers' and collectors' overs and shorts are reported to management for action where necessary.
3.10 The transfers from National Giro and ensure that the control exercised over both cleared and uncleared remittances is adequate.
3.11 That transfers received from bank Giros are adequately recorded and controlled.
3.12 The summary of collections and ensure that control is adequate.
3.13 That the system for credit posting is adequately controlled and that any unposted/unidentified cash is recorded and controlled.

GENERAL

3.14 Examine and ensure that the system of cash collection by agencies is adequate and that bankings are made without delay.

3.15 Ascertain that National Giro and night safe facilities are used in order to reduce the cash held overnight.

3.16 Examine arrangements for the banking of cash collections under contract security services.

3.17 Verify, in cases where payments can be made from collections, that these are adequately covered by documentation.

3.18 Verify, where cash is paid over from one cashier/collector to a supervisor, etc., that there is a clear indication of the discharge of responsibility.

4.   *Main areas of internal control*

4.1   It should be the responsibility of an independent person to control the stocks and daily usage of manual type receipts.

4.2   There should be control over receipts issued by both receipt books and receipting machines.

4.3   There should be a reconciliation of daily collections and bankings.

4.4   The system should provide for any cash in hand and unbanked from the previous day to be isolated and to be seen to be banked.

4.5   Cheque payments should be identified to obviate 'teeming and lading'.

4.6   The system should provide for the 'crossing' of cheques, postal orders, etc., when received.

Basic audit programme

TRAVELLING AND SUBSISTENCE ALLOWANCES

1. *Objectives*

To ensure that allowances for the use of employees' private cars on the organisation's business, and subsistence claims, are properly authorised, and that payments are made in accordance with the organisation's scheme.

2. *Area of audit*

2.1 Commences with approval as an authorised or casual user.
2.2 Finishes with payment to the employee.

3. *Basic programme*

CONTROL

3.1 To review and test the procedures for the authorisation of payment of travelling and subsistence allowances and the verification of current insurance.
3.2 To review and test the procedures for the submission of claims for mileage incurred and subsistence claimed.

CLAIMS

By sample, verify the following:

3.3 That the vehicle for which the car allowance is claimed is registered in the name of the officer concerned. (This check will have to be done via the Driving Vehicle Licensing Centre at Swansea to obtain the name and address of the owner from the registration documents.)
3.4 That the essential user or casual user is properly authorised.
3.5 That the vehicle cubic capacity agrees with the registration details.
3.6 The reasonableness of the claim and also check that it is properly completed in accordance with instructions.
3.7 That a claim is properly authorised by an approved officer.
3.8 That the rate per mile, lump sum (where applicable) and subsistence allowance are correct.
3.9 That the calculations are correct.
3.10 Where speedo. readings are available from a supplementary source of information, confirm that some private mileage is incurred each day and at weekends. In other words, there should be gaps between the speedo. readings shown one day for official use and another.
3.11 The payment to employees.

GENERAL

3.12 Examine for nil mileages and enquire into reasons.
3.13 Review the need for essential user status where little mileage is incurred.

4.   *Main areas of internal control*

4.1   Procedures are provided for proper authorisation of essential and casual users.

4.2   Claims are submitted that show details of the mileage incurred, the subsistence claimed and the reasons which enable authorising officers to approve.

4.3   The approval of claims is given by designated officers.

4.4   Management information is provided to enable the scheme to be kept under review and also to bring cases, where low mileages or large mileages are claimed, to the attention of chief officers, for re-appraisal of authorisation.

Basic audit programme

TRANSPORT

1. *Objectives*

To verify the following:

1.1 That proper management controls operate regarding the purchasing, leasing, hire and disposal of vehicles and plant.
1.2 That the cost of repair and maintenance programmes is being effectively monitored.
1.3 That control is being exercised over vehicle and plant running costs, including fuel, tyres, batteries and spare parts.
1.4 That control is being exercised over the utilisation of vehicles and plant.
1.5 That the computerised vehicle job costing system recharge to service departments is working satisfactorily.

2. *Area of audit*

2.1 Commences with vehicle acquisition.
2.2 Finishes with vehicle disposal.

3. *Basic programme*

ACQUISITION AND DISPOSAL OF VEHICLES AND PLANT

3.1 Review procedures for authorisation of addition/replacement vehicles.
3.2 Review procedures for disposal of vehicles no longer required.

By sample, verify the following:

3.3 That all purchases of new vehicles are authorised in accordance with procedures.
3.4 That reasons for additional/replacement vehicles are valid in accordance with policy.
3.5 Tenders received for purchase of vehicles.
3.6 That disposal of vehicles are displaced in accordance with procedures.
3.7 That credit is received for disposed vehicles.
3.8 The plant register entries and depreciation rates or entries in the leasing register.

HIRED VEHICLES

For a sample period, verify the following:

3.9 That hire is authorised in accordance with policy.
3.10 That quotations for hire are obtained.
3.11 That rates and details of hire invoices are correct.
3.12 That economic use is being made of hired vehicles i.e., that vehicles are not idle whilst hired transport in use.

MAINTENANCE OF VEHICLES

3.13 Review the policy for servicing and repairs.

Inspect a sample of vehicle history records to verify the following:

3.14 That servicing is carried out regularly in accordance with the programme.

3.15 That planned inspection of vehicles is carried out in accordance with the programme.

3.16 That where repairs or maintenance are carried out by outside firms, this is in accordance with policy.

3.17 That the MOT test requirements are met.

3.18 The extent of supervisory checks on work done (both by own labour and outside firms).

3.19 That insurance claims are made in case of accident damage.

3.20 That the system for recording expenditure and maintenance is operating satisfactorily.

3.21 Compare charges/costs for jobs with the standard charges of private garages.

VEHICLE RUNNING

By sample, verify the following:

3.22 The use of agency cards and petrol purchases from outside garages. Also verify that the receipts and issues of petrol, derv and oil from stocks are properly controlled and recorded.

3.23 That tyre requirements are in accordance with arrangements.

3.24 That the issue of vehicle spares, etc., from stocks and direct purchases are properly controlled and recorded, paying particular attention to attractive items.

3.25 That tax and insurance charges and appropriate refunds are obtained.

3.26 That drivers' record books are properly completed.

USE OF VEHICLES

3.27 Appraise supervisory arrangements.

3.28 Examine arrangements for routing vehicles, delivery areas, etc.

3.29 Appraise suitability of vehicle used.

3.30 Appraise and test procedures for authorising vehicles to be taken home.

3.31 Examine use of cars and verify recharge to users where appropriate.

3.32 Review and assess time spent 'off the road' and the reasons therefore.

3.33 Examine vehicle use statistics and test the accuracy of management information.

GARAGING

3.34 Appraise adequacy of premises.

3.35 Appraise security arrangements.

3.36 Examine custody of spares and tools.

4.   *Main areas of internal control*

4.1 In addition to normal expenditure authorisation procedures, there should be a system of request and justification for additional or hired vehicles reviewed by the transport manager.

4.2 The system should provide for review and justification of the continued hiring of vehicles.

4.3 There should be a recognised policy for disposal of vehicles and a control that the appropriate credits are received.

4.4 Proper procedures should exist for the regular obtaining of quotations for hire.

4.5 Adequate records should be kept to ensure vehicles are called forward for servicing and for their inspection to comply with legislative requirements.

4.6 Proper control should be exercised over the purchase and issue of fuel stocks and of the use of agency cards. Independent dippings of fuel stocks held should be carried out regularly and any discrepancies certified by a designated officer.

4.7 Proper control should be exercised over spares, tyres and other stocks.

4.8 Suitable management information should be prepared to enable a constant review of utilisation and costs of the fleet to be carried out.

Examples of internal control questionnaires

Internal control questionnaire

EXPENDITURE

	Yes	No	Comments

Obtain the financial regulations regarding expenditure.

1. *Budget estimates*
1.1 Do financial regulations provide for the preparation of:
   (*a*) Capital estimates:
      (i) Over a period of more than one year?
      (ii) Over a period of more than three years?
   (*b*) Revenue estimates for more than one year?
1.2 Is virement allowed?
   If so:
   (*a*) Is there a procedure specified for its control?
   (*b*) Is there a limit on the amount of virement from any one expenditure head?
1.3 Do financial regulations provide for:
   (*a*) Application for supplement-ary estimates?
      If so:
      (i) Is there a specified procedure?

Yes	No	Comments

(ii) Is there a limit
below which committee
approval is not required?

(b) An inflation reserve?
If so, is there a procedure laid
down for the control and
allocation of the reserve?

(c) Specific approval in addition
to budget approval for
certain categories of
expenditure?
If so, which expenditure?

1.4 Do financial regulations specify
which categories of revenue
expenditure should be subject to
the submission of a financial
implications report?

1.5 Is a financial implications report
on revenue costs required for
proposed capital projects?

1.6 Is the spending department
responsible for budgetary
control?

1.7 Are regular statements of expenditure against estimates supplied
to spending departments?

1.8 Is the chief financial officer
responsible for notifying spending departments when:
(a) Actual expenditure
approaches estimate?
(b) Actual expenditure exceeds
estimate?
Is action taken at stage (b)?

1.9 Have estimate headings been
agreed with the spending
departments?
If so, are they in the same form as
the expenditure analysis
headings?

1.10 Are capital feasibility studies
undertaken?

	Yes	No	Comments

1.11 Is the chief financial officer responsible for reporting on the cost of capital works?
Is the spending department so responsible?
At what stage are reports submitted:
(*a*) Currently?
(*b*) When cost approaches estimate?
(*c*) When cost exceeds estimate?
(*d*) On completion of works?

1.12 Are major over/under spendings reported to the committee?
If so, is the report submitted by:
(*a*) The chief financial officer?
(*b*) The spending department?

1.13 Have the financial regulations been complied with?

2. *Tenders and quotations*
This would be covered in a Contracts ICQ.

3. *Ordering*

3.1 Is any distinction drawn between orders for supplies of a routine and recurring nature and orders for supplies of a special and non-recurring nature?

3.2 Is authority to order restricted to specified officers?
If so:
(*a*) Is a list of such officers maintained?
(*b*) Are orders actually signed by these officers?

3.3 Are order books controlled?

3.4 Is the signing officer responsible for receipt or custody of supplies?

3.5 Are orders supported by a written requisition?

3.6 Is the requisitioning officer responsible for receipt or custody of supplies?

	Yes	No	Comments

3.7 Does the order clearly indicate point of delivery?

3.8 Does the ordering officer satisfy himself of the necessity for the order?

3.9 Is a written order sent to the supplier in every case?

(*a*) Is the form of the order approved by the chief financial officer?

(*b*) Does the chief financial officer receive a copy of the order?
If so:

(i) Is this at the same time as the orders are despatched to suppliers?

(ii) Or is the copy order attached to the invoice when submitted for payment?

(*c*) Does any other person receive a copy of the order?

3.10 Which officers interview salesmen?

3.11 Does the department/ establishment record commitments against estimates?
If so, are financial analysis headings used?

3.12 Is there a procedure for dealing with verbal orders/emergency orders/open order, etc.?
If so, how often is it used?

3.13 Do order books have a unique prefix or reference which will enable the order to be traced to a department or establishment?

3.14 Are recommendations on the suitability of firms and their products made available to spending departments and establishments by a central purchasing officer?

	Yes	No	Comments

If so, are orders scrutinised to ensure that goods are obtained from recommended sources?

3.15 Is a time for retention of copy orders specified?

3.16 Is special attention paid to orders which might cover 'inertia selling' practices, i.e. orders for carbon paper, paint, stock orders, etc.?

3.17 Are orders 'marked off' when completed?

4. *Receipt of goods*

4.1 Is the receipt of goods authenticated by:
(*a*) Receipted delivery notes?
(*b*) Signed goods inward sheets?
(*c*) Any other method?

4.2 Are delivery notes or any other stationery recording delivery retained?
If so, is a period of retention specified?

4.3 Are goods checked on delivery as to:
(*a*) Quality?
(*b*) Quantity?

4.4 Is there a procedure specified in respect of:
(*a*) Rejected deliveries?
(*b*) Partial deliveries?
(*c*) Over/under deliveries?
(*d*) Goods on 'approval'?

4.5 Are reports submitted to a responsible officer (e.g. central purchasing officer), in respect of:
(*a*) Poor quality?
(*b*) Delays in deliveries?
(*c*) Incomplete deliveries?
(*d*) Substitution for 'out of stock' items?
If so, is appropriate action taken by him?

	Yes	No	Comments

4.6 Is there adequate security for goods once they have been received?

4.7 Has someone the sole responsibility for custody and issue of stocks?

5. *Confirmation of work done*

   Is evidence of satisfactory performance of work done, or services supplied, obtained prior to the relevant invoices being certified?

6. *Invoice certification and check*

6.1 Which invoice system is used:
   (*a*) 'Official'?
   If so, is it adequately controlled?
   (*b*) Suppliers?

6.2 Do financial regulations prescribe the officers authorised to certify invoices?
   If so:
   (*a*) Is a current list of signatures maintained?
   (*b*) Are amendments approved?

6.3 Are invoices actually certified by these officers?

6.4 Is the certification by facsimile signature?
   If so, are the facsimile stamps in safe custody?

6.5 Does the certifying officer:
   (*a*) Order supplies?
   (*b*) Receive supplies?

6.6 Is there a common invoice grid certification stamp?
   (i) Is it stamped on the invoice?
   (ii) Or is it a stick-on certification slip?
   Does it provide for:
   (*a*) The reference to specific approval?

	Yes	No	Comments

(*b*) That a specific order number is marked off?

(*c*) That the receipted delivery note or weigh ticket is checked?

(*d*) That the work is satisfactorily completed?

(*e*) That prices and discounts are checked?

(*f*) The minute reference?

(*g*) That the arithmetic has been checked?

(*h*) The certification by chief officer?

(*i*) The expenditure coding and creditor coding?

(*j*) The reference to inventory or stores ledger?

(*k*) The examination by the chief financial officer?

(*l*) That the account has not previously been certified for payment?

(*m*) The invoice reference?

(*n*) The VAT allocation?

6.7 Is there a specified procedure for the payment of copy invoices?

6.8 Are copy orders endorsed as to the date invoices are submitted to the chief financial officer for payment?

6.9 Are copy orders marked off on receipt of invoices?
If yes, by whom?

6.10 Does the payments procedure give special treatment to invoices:
(*a*) Over a certain amount?
(*b*) Subject to prompt payment discount?

6.11 Is there a record of recurring payments?
If so, is the record held in:
(*a*) The chief financial officer's department?

	Yes	No	Comments

(*b*) The spending department?
(*c*) Both?

6.12 Is there a procedure for dealing with urgent payments?
If so, is there machinery for:
    (i) Avoiding duplicate payments?
    (ii) Ensuring that all urgent payments are properly authorised?

6.13 Are supplier statements examined?
If so, by whom?

6.14 Are certified statements refused for payment?

7. *Analysis of expenditure*

7.1 Who codes the invoices:
(*a*) The establishment?
(*b*) The spending department?
(*c*) The finance department?

7.2 If the organisation or spending department is responsible for coding invoices, is the coding checked by the chief financial officer?

7.3 If the finance department is responsible for coding invoices, is there a separate person responsible for the scrutiny of the coding?

7.4 Is expenditure analysed by machine process? If so, is the reconciliation of totals the responsibility of someone not involved in the machine process?

7.5 Is expenditure analysed manually?
If so, is the reconciliation carried out by someone not involved in the actual analysis?

	Yes	No	Comments

8.   *Outstanding creditors*

8.1   Do departments prepare lists of outstanding creditors and send them to the chief financial officers:
(a) At the year end?
(b) At other times?

8.2   Are these examined by the chief financial officers?

9.   *General*

9.1   Do manuals of guidance exist for staff engaged in the payment of invoices in:
(a) The establishment?
(b) The spending department?
(c) The finance department?
If so, have they been revised within the last two years?

9.2   Are the duties of staff separated so that internal check requirements are fulfilled?

9.3   Are the duties of staff involved in the payment of invoices periodically rotated?

9.4   Do staff involved in the payment of invoices:
(a) Take all their leave?
(b) Complete their duties without working regular overtime?

9.5   Are staff engaged in the payment of invoices covered by adequate fidelity guarantee insurance?

9.6   Is there a review procedure for errors located both before and after payment?
(a) Is the person who performs this review not engaged in the payment of creditors?
(b) Is a record of errors maintained and periodically examined by a senior member of staff?

	Yes	No	Comments

(c) Are manual alterations allowed for in the system? If so, at what points?

10.   *Travelling expenses and subsistence allowance claims*

10.1 Are travelling expenses claims:
      (a) Submitted regularly?
      (b) Completed correctly?
      (c) Certified properly?

10.2 Do departments have satis-factory arrangements for:
      (a) Authorising journeys?
      (b) Checking mileages claimed?
      (c) Ensuring economic use of vehicles?

10.3 (a) Is the cubic capacity of the car shown?
      (b) Has the correct mileage rate been paid?

10.4 Are the mileages claimed reasonable?

10.5 Is the purpose of each journey claimed compatible with the individual's post?

10.6 Is the period of absence from the individual's base sufficient to justify claiming subsistence allowance?

10.7 Have any passengers shown on the claim also claimed for the same journey?

Internal control questionnaire

BANK AND CASH TRANSACTIONS

	Yes	No	Comments
1. *Bank accounts*			
Obtain details of all main and subsidiary bank accounts, with full titles, account numbers and authorised signatories.			
1.1 (*a*) Is there a written statement of bank terms agreed by the organisation's bankers?			
(*b*) Have bank terms been reviewed within a reasonable period (say two to three years)?			
1.2 Are there instructions covering the use and operation of bank accounts in: (*a*) The organisation? (*b*) The department?			
1.3 Are all these accounts in the name of the organisation?			
1.4 Has the bank been instructed not to open further accounts without proper authority?			
1.5 Do bank terms specify overdraft arrangements on the various accounts?			
1.6 What action has the bank been instructed to take if any subsidiary account becomes overdrawn?			
1.7 Has the bank been instructed on limits (e.g. as to amount payable on one signature) on all accounts?			
1.8 Is money released from the main bank account only to fund subsidiary accounts out of which external payments are made? If so, have instructions been issued covering funding methods?			

	Yes	No	Comments

1.9   If any cheques are drawn on the main account, are there safeguards as to authorisation and signatures?

1.10 Are there similar safeguards for transfers to subsidiary accounts?

1.11 Are there safeguards in respect of direct debits?

1.12 Are there arrangements for controlling 'cash flow'?
If so, is a specific officer responsible?

1.13 Is a responsible officer checking the bank's calculations re.:
(*a*) Bank interest?
(*b*) Bank charges?

1.14 Are all subsidiary funds operated on an imprest basis?

1.15 Are the amounts/existence/ needs of the imprests reviewed periodically?

1.16 Is satisfactory evidence of outgoings produced before the accounts are reimbursed?

2.   *Cheque control*

2.1   (*a*) Has the person who orders cheques any other part in the payment procedure?
(*b*) Is there an indemnity from the printer regarding the fraudulent use of cheques?

2.2   Are all cheques stored in safe custody?

2.3   Are all cheque forms issued to approved identified personnel and acknowledged in writing?

2.4   Is the stock balance of cheque forms verified:
(*a*) Daily?
(*b*) Weekly?

	Yes	No	Comments

2.5 Are 'open' cheques used?
If so:
  (*a*) Is there a limit on the
     amount?
  (*b*) Is their use restricted to
     specified purposes?

2.6 Is the number of cheques used
reconciled with the number of
authorised payments by a person
independent of the payments
system?

2.7 (*a*) Are records maintained of
     spoiled and cancelled
     cheques?
  (*b*) Are the cheques returned to
     internal audit?

2.8 Do cheque writing procedures
for normal and urgent payments
differ?

2.9 Where cheques are signed in
manuscript:
  (*a*) Are two signatories
     required?
  (*b*) Is the amount under one
     signature limited?

2.10 Where a cheque-signing machine
is in use:
  (*a*) Are the key and the dies held
     by a responsible officer?
  (*b*) Is the number of cheques
     signed, recorded and agreed
     with the number of cheques
     issued?
  (*c*) Is a manuscript initial made
     on the cheque?
  (*d*) Is such an initial a condition
     of payment by the bank?
  (*e*) Has the bank accepted
     instructions to this effect?
  (*f*) Is the amount of any one
     cheque limited?

	Yes	No	Comments

2.11 Where pre-signed cheques are used:
 (a) Is a manuscript initial and/or rubber stamp made on the cheque?
 (b) Is the authority to do this restricted?
 (c) Is this a condition of payment by the bank?
 (d) Has the bank accepted instructions to this effect?
 (e) Is the amount of any one cheque limited?
 (f) Is there a limit above which a manuscript signature is also required?
 (g) Is there an indemnity from printers re. misuse?

2.12 Where signature is by rubber stamp:
 (a) Is the stamp holder a responsible officer and does he store the stamp in a secure place?
 (b) Is a manuscript initial made on the cheque?
 (c) Is such an initial a condition of payment by the bank?
 (d) Has the bank accepted instructions to this effect?
 (e) Is the amount of any one cheque limited?

2.13 Is there a procedure for opening crossed cheques?
 (a) Is the authority to open cheques restricted to specified officers?
 (b) Do instructions specify under what circumstances a cheque can be opened?

2.14 (a) Is there a procedure specified for the preparation of cheques for despatch?

	Yes	No	Comments

(*b*) Are all people involved in despatch independent of the payments procedures?

(*c*) Is a record kept of all cheques not despatched immediately to the creditor?

(*d*) Is proof of identity and a signature required from creditors who collect their cheques?

(*e*) Are the cheques kept secure until they are handed to the Post Office?

2.15 Is there a procedure for handling returned cheques and recording them past the letter opening stage?

(*a*) Is any independent authority required to authorise the re-issue of cheques?

2.16 When duplicate cheques are issued, is an indemnity required from the payee?

2.17 Is there a facility to stop cheques?
If so, is it controlled?

2.18 Are alterations to cheques permitted?
If so, are they controlled?

2.19 Is a fidelity guarantee in force with adequate cover for defalcations concerning cheques?

3.   *Reconciliation*

Do reconciliation procedures provide for:

3.1 The designation of an officer responsible for bank reconciliation?
If so, is he independent of preparation and despatch of cheques?

3.2 A set frequency for obtaining paid cheques from the bank?

	Yes	No	Comments

3.3 The intervals at which reconciliations must be effected?

3.4 The requirements concerning authorisation for writing back unpresented cheques?

3.5 The reconciliation of payments with expenditure analysis?

3.6 A procedure to be followed in the event of errors arising?

4. *Petty cash, postage and minor disbursement accounts*

Obtain details of all accounts which are in existence.

4.1 Do regulations provide that persons responsible for operating accounts are individually specified by name and post and notified to the chief financial officer?

4.2 Are accounts which must be kept on an imprest basis specified?

4.3 Are payments restricted to account holders only?

4.4 Is there a limit on the amount of any one payment?

4.5 Are account holders personally responsible for custody of cash (stamps)?

4.6 Must bank accounts be opened when the amount held is over defined limits?

4.7 Is access to cash (stamps) limited to account holders?

4.8 Are overdrafts on bank accounts prohibited?

4.9 Are advances/reimbursements made only on receipt of supporting evidence?

4.10 Are acknowledgements from account holders required at specific intervals?

	Yes	No	Comments
4.11 Are cash balances checked periodically by persons other than account holders? If so, are balances and dates recorded?			
4.12 Are any accounts funded by round sum advances? If so, are there rules governing the authorisation and control of such advances?			
4.13 Has an officer been designated as being responsible for determining the total advance to be held by each individual account holder?			

Internal control questionnaire

STORES AND STOCKTAKING

Statistics

Period	No. of receipts	No. of issues	Stock at		Annual turnover £
			No. of items	Value £	

	Name(s)	Location
Storekeeper(s).		
Officer with overall control of stores system.		
Officer responsible for stocktaking.		
Accounting records kept by:		
Bin card. Stores ledger – manual. Stores ledger – mechanical. Issue transfer and return notes.		
Goods received notes. Stock adjustment notes. Order books. Copy orders. Invoices. Computer.		

	Method	Date last completed
Stocktaking procedure.		
Stock valuation basis.		

	Yes	No	Comments

1. *Security*

1.1 Was auditor asked to show any identification prior to access?

1.2 Is there a controlled access point?

1.3 Do premises appear secure against intruders?

1.4 Can storekeepers observe all exits?
If 'no', is any improvement possible?

1.5 Is the storekeeper the only key holder?
(If 'no', list other keyholders.)
Are the keys kept in a safe place?

1.6 Is the storekeeper the only person allowed to receive and issue stores?
If 'no', give details.

1.7 Is there adequate control of the goods inwards bay in order to prevent pilfering by visiting delivery people?

1.8 Is it possible for unauthorised persons to collect goods from the dispatch bay?

1.9 Can control of either bay be improved?
If 'yes', give details.

1.10 Is the store and its contents adequately insured for loss?

2. *Fuel*

2.1 Does the storekeeper control vehicle fuel stocks?

2.2 Are fuel pumps and inlets locked when not in use?

2.3 Do drivers sign for fuel issues?

2.4 Are vehicle registration numbers recorded on the issue sheets?

2.5 Are fuel pump meter readings recorded on issue sheets?

2.6 When were pumps last checked for accuracy of quantity delivered and recorded?

	Yes	No	Comments

2.7 Is dipping done at regular
     intervals by a person other than
     the storekeeper?

2.8 Are tolerance levels allowed?
     If 'yes', specify.

2.9 Are statistics of level of issues
     prepared?

2.10 Do these show the trend of issues
     you would expect?
     Is this reviewed regularly?

2.11 Are there adequate arrange-
     ments for recharging other
     authorised users?

3.   *Ordering*

3.1 Are official orders used for stores
     items in all cases?

3.2 Are verbal orders permitted in
     an emergency only?
     Does the system ensure that
     written confirmation follows by
     next working day?

3.3 Is the person signing orders:
     (*a*) Authorised to do so?
     (*b*) Independent of the store-
          keeper?

3.4 Does the storekeeper initiate
     requisitions for orders?

3.5 Does the storekeeper get a copy
     of the order?

3.6 Are orders issued only to
     approved suppliers, in accord-
     ance with buying policy?

3.7 Are they within any authorised
     limits laid down by the
     organisation?

3.8 Are the net prices obtained, the
     lowest possible?
     If 'no', give any other deciding
     factors (i.e. delivery date, etc.).

3.9 How often are suppliers asked to
     tender?

3.10 Who interviews salesmen
     wishing to supply stock items?

	Yes	No	Comments

3.11 Are maximum/re-order/
minimum levels of stock laid
down?

3.12 Are these levels regularly
reviewed?

4.   *Receipts*

4.1   Are all deliveries checked,
before acceptance, to:
(*a*) Delivery notes?
(*b*) Copy orders?
If 'no', is the delivery note
marked to show 'subject to a
detailed check'?

4.2   Are all bulk materials weighed
before being accepted, or is an
official weigh ticket produced?

4.3   Is the system for part deliveries
adequate?

4.4   Are goods received notes
prepared?

4.5   Are all goods received promptly
recorded and taken into store?

4.6   Is the recording of goods
received independent of the
checking of invoices?

4.7   Is the person certifying the
invoice as to goods received:
(*a*) Authorised to do so?
(*b*) Independent of the
storekeeper?

4.8   Are there adequate procedures
to ensure:
(*a*) Return of goods to suppliers?
(*b*) Claims for shortages,
breakages and incorrect
deliveries?
(*c*) All credit notes received?
(*d*) Return and control of
chargeable containers, etc.?

5.   *Issues*

5.1   Are requisitions/issue notes
completed for all issues being
made?

	Yes	No	Comments
5.2 Are requisitions/issue notes correctly made out and authorised by persons who are not storekeepers?			
5.3 Are requisitions/issue notes examined for reasonableness of quantities? If so: (*a*) By whom? (*b*) At what stage?			
5.4 Is there a list of persons who are authorised to sign requisitions/ issue notes?			
5.5 Does the storekeeper know who is authorised to sign requisitions/ issue notes?			
5.6 Does the recipient sign for all items received?			
5.7 Are all bulk materials weighed before issue?			
5.8 Are the procedures in respect of unfulfilled requisitions/issue notes satisfactory?			
5.9 Are arrangements for 'emergency' or 'night shift' issues adequate?			
6. *Returns/transfers*			
6.1 Are goods returned notes used for: (*a*) Unused items? (*b*) Second-hand items? (*c*) Scrap?			
6.2 Does the person who authorises the issues make out a goods returned note? If 'no', detail.			
6.3 Does the storekeeper acknowledge the receipt of items returned?			
6.4 Are second-hand stores kept separate from new items?			
6.5 Are transfers between stores properly documented?			

	Yes	No	Comments

6.6 Are goods returned promptly recorded and taken into store?

6.7 Is the level of returns unduly high?

7. *Sales*

7.1 Are sales allowed?

7.2 Are sales restricted to particular items?
If 'yes', specify.

7.3 Are sales restricted to certain categories of persons?
If so, are sales made only to these categories of person?

7.4 Are the sales properly documented?

7.5 (*a*) Is the authority's policy of charging being adhered to?
(*b*) Are sales prices adequate to ensure no financial loss to the organisation?

7.6 Are competitive tenders invited for the sale of scrap?

7.7 Is cash received/sale authorised by a person independent of the storekeeper?

7.8 Does the storekeeper ensure that the payment is received and the sale authorised before goods are issued?

8. *Accounting records*

8.1 Where stores records are posted from prime documents, are there arrangements to ensure that all such documents are accounted for?

8.2 Is the ledger updated at intervals not greater than those specified by management?

8.3 Are adequate measures taken to ensure that the ledger shows an up-to-date position?

	Yes	No	Comments

8.4 Are the procedures for dealing with the following satisfactory from the point of view of authorisation and correct recording?
  (*a*) Additional new stock items (including allocation of commodity codes).
  (*b*) Deletion of stock items.
  And, where applicable:
  (*c*) Adjustment of prices.
  (*d*) Adjustment of unit of issue.
  (*e*) Adjustment of minimum or maximum stock levels.
  (*f*) Adjustment of re-order quantities.

8.5 (*a*) Are items of small value treated as consumable?
  (*b*) Is a list kept of these items?
  (*c*) Is this list reviewed at regular intervals?

8.6 Is there any duplication of manual and computer records? If 'yes', give details.

9. *Stocktaking*

9.1 Is stocktaking carried out independently of the storekeeper/stores control check?

9.2 Are all stock checks supported by stock taking sheets? If 'yes', are stocks checked:
  (*a*) Continuously?
  (*b*) At set intervals?

9.3 Are all items checked at least once every year?

9.4 (*a*) Are attractive and valuable items checked at least monthly?
  (*b*) Is the level of shortages in this area high, either in number or value?

9.5 Are all discrepancies investigated and reported on? If so, by whom?

	Yes	No	Comments

9.6 Are all write-offs properly authorised?

9.7 (*a*) Is the ledger adjusted for discrepancies immediately the authority to do so is given?

(*b*) Is the control of the disposal of obsolete items adequate?

(*c*) Are tenders invited in appropriate cases for the disposal of such items?

10. *Management information*

10.1 Does the system provide for, *inter alia*:

(*a*) Information on slow moving/ obsolete items at regular intervals?

(*b*) Review of maximum/ minimum levels and re-order levels?

(*c*) Details of stock levels held on comparative dates?

10.2 Is appropriate action taken on management information produced?

10.3 (*a*) Does a procedure manual exist?

(*b*) Have all the staff concerned got copies?

(*c*) When was it last reviewed?

11. *Inventories*

11.1 Is an inventory kept? If so, has the head of the establishment a copy of the instructions regarding inventories?

11.2 Has a stock check of equipment been carried out within the last 12 months? If so:

(*a*) By whom?

(*b*) Is there satisfactory evidence of this?

Yes	No	Comments

11.3 Have recently purchased articles been entered in the inventory?

11.4 Are serial numbers and/or types of relatively valuable articles entered in the inventory?

11.5 (*a*) Has a list been kept of the number and value of trophies/cups?
(*b*) Are they covered by insurance?

11.6 Have details of gifts been reported to managers/governors and recorded on the inventory?

11.7 Are there any items which the head of the organisation regards as surplus to requirements?

11.8 Has any income arisen from write-offs and disposals and has it been brought into account?

11.9 Have all write-offs been properly authorised?

11.10 Is any form of identification marking (e.g. identification paint) used?
If so, has it been applied to all relevant items?

11.11 Is a copy of the inventory held elsewhere?

General comments regarding the system

1. Do you consider:
   (*a*) The store is necessary?
   (*b*) The store is cost effective?
   (*c*) The store is correctly located?
   (*d*) The general layout and operation of the store to be efficient?
   (*e*) The number of staff to be too high/too low/correct?
   (*f*) The general competence of the staff to be high/low/ adequate?
2. Any other comments.

Internal control questionnaire

CONTROL OF INCOME

	Yes	No	Comments
1. *Postal remittances*			
1.1 Are remittances ever received by post? If 'yes':			
1.2 Is post received through a post box?			
1.3 If post box is used, is it locked? If so, does it have two locks operated by different keys?			
1.4 Are keys to the post box properly controlled in that they are held by separate people?			
1.5 (*a*) Does more than one person clear the post box? (*b*) Is the mail delivered directly and quickly to the post openers?			
1.6 Can the contents be removed from the post box by un-authorised persons? (In other words, is the aperture too large and is the lock adequate?)			
1.7 Can the post box be removed complete with contents?			
1.8 If a post box is not used: (*a*) How is the post received? (*b*) By whom is it received? (*c*) Is the post opened immediately? (*d*) If not, is it kept securely?			
1.9 Does more than one person open the post?			
1.10 Who supervises the post opening procedure?			
1.11 Does the cashier assist in the opening of post?			
1.12 Do postal remittances consist of: (*a*) Cheques, MOs, POs? (*b*) Cash?			

	Yes	No	Comments

1.13 Are all remittances other than cash immediately crossed to the bank account by the post opening staff?

1.14 Are all remittances recorded immediately in a remittance record, giving details of payer, amount paid and type of remittance?
If not, are cash remittances recorded?

1.15 At what time are remittance records prepared?

1.16 Does the supervisor sign these records?

1.17 Are remittance records totalled and agreed with remittances before they leave the section where the post is opened?

1.18 Once the post has been opened, are all remittances immediately handed to:
(*a*) The cashier?
(*b*) Other departments as appropriate?
(*c*) Any other person?

1.19 Are discharges received?

1.20 Is a satisfactory system in operation for dealing with post-dated or incorrectly made out cheques, or misaddressed remittances?

1.21 Are receipts issued for:
(*a*) All postal remittances including cheques?
(*b*) Cheques on request only?

1.22 If yes, are these issued:
(*a*) By the staff opening the post, when it is opened?
(*b*) At a later stage?

1.23 Is there a procedure for dealing with unidentified remittances?
If so:
(*a*) Is the system satisfactory?

	Yes	No	Comments

(*b*) Are appropriate steps taken to identify such remittances?

1.24 Are receipts agreed to remittance records:
(*a*) In total?
(*b*) Individually?
If so, by whom?

1.25 Is all recorded and registered mail signed for by a senior assistant and recorded in a registered post book?
If so:
(*a*) Are the packets opened under supervision?
(*b*) Are the contents entered into the registered post book?

1.26 If the answer to para. 1.25 is 'no', how is the registered and recorded mail dealt with?

1.27 Are all the remittances received during the day, which do not require a receipt, placed in a · suitably marked receptacle by the payer?
If 'yes':
(*a*) Is this opened by more than one person?
(*b*) Are such remittances dealt with by the normal post opening system?

1.28 If the answer to para. 1.27 is 'no', how are remittances received during the day, which do not require a receipt, dealt with?

1.29 Does anyone associated with the receipt of income handle accountancy records?

2.   *Remittances received by staff*

2.1 (*a*) Which staff, other than cashiers, receive remittances?
(*b*) Is this in the normal course of their duty?

	Yes	No	Comments

(c) If not, how often do they receive remittances and why?

2.2 Do these staff:
  (a) Issue official receipts?
  (b) Keep a record of all remittances received?
  (c) Remit at regular intervals?
  (d) Remit cash intact?

2.3 Are the staff's records reconciled with paying-in records?

2.4 By whom?

2.5 Are issues of paying-in books controlled?

2.6 Security of cash – see Section 13.

2.7 Are official sums banked/paid to the finance department:
  (a) Weekly?
  (b) More than once a week?
  (c) Less than once a week?
  If (c), are the reasons for this satisfactory?

2.8 Who normally visits the bank/finance department to pay in money?
  (a) Are routes and times regularly varied?
  (b) Is an escort provided?

2.9 Is a maximum sum for overnight retention fixed for each collecting employee?

2.10 Does the person in charge know of the insurance position regarding:
  (a) Cash in transit?
  (b) The use of private cars by members of staff on official business?

3.   *Receipting systems*

3.1 Are all remittances receipted? If not, specify reasons.

3.2 What method of receipting is employed:
  (a) Manually written receipts with carbon copy?

	Yes	No	Comments

(*b*) Manually written receipts without carbon copy?

(*c*) Cash registers or receipting machines?

(*d*) Visual display units?

(*e*) Sales notes, tickets or similiar documents?

(*f*) Other means? (Specify details.)

3.3 Are manually produced receipts made out in ink?

3.4 Does the person who receives the money, sign or initial in his own name?

3.5 Are carbon copies kept?
If so:
(*a*) How many?
(*b*) By whom are they kept?

3.6 Are all copies of cancelled receipts retained?
If so:
(*a*) Who retains them?
(*b*) Is there a procedure for their eventual destruction?

3.7 Is all receipting stationery controlled by a section independent of the cashier's section?

4.   *Cash registers and receipting machines*

4.1 Give details of make and number of each cash register or receipting machine in use at this location.

4.2 Are till roll totals reconciled daily to cash takings and recorded in a permanent register?

4.3 (*a*) Are dates and reset numbers recorded on the till rolls at the end of each day's operations?
If so, by whom?

	Yes	No	Comments

(*b*) Is this operation carried out by a person independently of the machine operator?
If so, by whom?

4.4 Is access to the register reset operation and till roll restricted?
If so:
(*a*) Is it restricted to the person who carries out the operation in para. 4.3?
(*b*) Does he/she retain the key?

4.5 Are old till rolls retained for inspection?

4.6 For how long are they retained?

4.7 Are the keys to the machine properly controlled?

4.8 How many cashiers can use each machine?

4.9 Can each cashier's takings be reconciled separately?
If so, is there a system for overs and unders?

4.10 Are details of the amount paid visible to the payer?

4.11 Does the person paying receive a receipt or other form of acknowledgement?

4.12 Are any other receptacles used to collect and hold cash?

4.13 What records are kept of cash registers or receipting machines:
(*a*) In use?
(*b*) In reserve?

4.14 Is any analysis of income produced by the machine?

4.15 If so, in what form?

5. *Collectors' registers (e.g. rent collectors)*

5.1 Are any monies collected by means of collectors' registers?
If so, specify.

5.2 Are stocks of stationery adequately controlled?

	Yes	No	Comments

5.3   Are the main accounting records maintained independently from the collector?

5.4   Are independent checks carried out to ensure that prime records held by debtors agree with official records?

6.   *Income where no receipt is given (e.g. confectionery sales and coin boxes)*

6.1   Is cash collected from coin boxes (e.g. telephones, hair-dryers and games):
(*a*) Regularly?
(*b*) By two people, if there is no meter?
(*c*) Paid over to the cashier?
(*d*) Subsequently compared with expenditure on the equipment?

6.2   Is an adequate record of the takings kept?

6.3   Is the cash paid over regularly?

If applicable:

6.4   Are regular stock checks carried out by an independent person?

6.5   Is income regularly evaluated from stock records, invoices, etc., and reconciled to expenditure?

6.6   Are profit ratios examined critically at regular intervals in order to establish whether a satisfactory return is being obtained?

7.   *Tickets*

7.1   For what purpose are tickets used?

7.2   (*a*) Are the tickets pre-numbered for each purpose?
(*b*) Is a register kept of their issue?

	Yes	No	Comments

7.3 How are tickets issued:
   (*a*) By machine?
      If 'yes', specify.
   (*b*) By hand?
      If 'yes', by whom?

7.4 Are tickets surrendered by the purchaser to a second officer?

7.5 If so, to whom?

7.6 Are tickets:
   (*a*) Cancelled and clipped?
   (*b*) Collected intact?

7.7 If collected intact, are they destroyed properly by a senior officer?

7.8 If a collecting ticket box is used, is it properly locked and controlled?

7.9 Are regular ticket inspections made?

7.10 If so, how frequently and by whom?

7.11 Are the tickets, etc., sold reconciled to the cash taken daily?

7.12 If so, by whom?

7.13 Is he independent of the person issuing the tickets?

7.14 Is a periodical reconciliation of the tickets, etc., issued to the establishment carried out?

7.15 By whom, and how does he evidence it?

7.16 Are prices shown on tickets?

7.17 If not:
   (*a*) Is the description wording both clear and adequate?
   (*b*) Are signboards satisfactorily worded and sited?

7.18 Are there adequate storage facilities for tickets?

8. *Sales notes*

8.1 For what purpose are sales notes issued?

	Yes	No	Comments

8.2 (*a*) Are they pre-numbered for each purpose?

(*b*) Is a register kept of their issue?

8.3 (*a*) How many copies are produced?

(*b*) How many copies are handed to the purchaser?

(*c*) How many copies are retained?

8.4 Are the goods to be purchased collected at another point? If so:

(*a*) How many copies of the sales note are relinquished by the purchaser?

(*b*) Is at least one copy retained by the person who issued it?

(*c*) Is the transfer of the goods acknowledged by the signature of the purchaser on the retained copy?

(*d*) Are stock records properly maintained?

(*e*) Are retained copies of the sales note properly filed?

8.5 If the answer to para. 8.4 is 'no', detail the system for the collection of goods and check the procedures.

9. *Visual display units*
This would be dealt with in a Computer ICQ.

10. *Other means of receipting*

10.1 Give details of any other means of receipting.

10.2 Is the internal check adequate?

11. *Payments to bank*

11.1 Are there instructions for the banking of income?

11.2 When are each day's takings banked?

11.3 Is all cash banked intact?

	Yes	No	Comments

11.4 Is the cash received used to make payments?

11.5 Is the preparation of the paying-in slip and the payment into the bank carried out with adequate separation of duties?

11.6 (*a*) Are all cheques banked in the next possible banking?

(*b*) Is the name of the establishment marked on the back of each cheque?

(*c*) Does the recording conform to the requirements of the Accounts and Audit Regulations (e.g. the cheques listed on the paying-in slip are referenced to receipt numbers)?

11.7 Is the total of all income received at the establishment reconciled to bankings in a satisfactory record (e.g. a C & D book)?

11.8 Are collections checked against the bank statement by persons independent from those involved in para. 11.5 above?

11.9 Are cheques not accepted by the bank, recorded and controlled upon their return to the organisation?

11.10 (*a*) Who has authority to instruct the bank to make adjustments between accounts?

(*b*) Is this satisfactory?

12. *Cashier*

12.1 Does the cashier have other cash-handling responsibilities? If so, specify.

12.2 Does the cashier have access to ledgers, accounts or write-offs?

12.3 (*a*) To whom does the cashier report any deficiencies?

	Yes	No	Comments

(*b*) Are they investigated immediately and properly recorded?

12.4 Has each cashier a separate till, and does he balance it separately?

12.5 Is the cashier responsible for processing bank credits?

12.6 Are satisfactory arrangements in operation to cover any absence of the cashier, including holidays?

13. *Security*

13.1 Is cash retained in the office overnight?

13.2 Is the amount held overnight kept to a minimum?

13.3 (*a*) What type and make(s) of safe does the organisation have?

(*b*) Is the safe properly anchored or installed?

(*c*) Is it of adequate strength and size?

(*d*) Does it conform to insurance requirements?

13.4 (*a*) Who holds the safe keys?

(*b*) Are they held by him/her personally?

(*c*) Who has knowledge of the combination lock numbers?

(*d*) Is the combination number written down anywhere?

(*e*) Has a copy of the combination numbers been deposited with a bank under security arrangements?

(*f*) Is the combination number changed at least once per annum?

	Yes	No	Comments

(g) Is the combination number changed after a member of staff with knowledge of the number leaves his/her employment?

13.5 (a) Is the person in charge aware of the limit of cash to be held overnight on the premises?

(b) Are all official monies held in the safe overnight?

(c) Is the person in charge aware of the insurance position relating to cash held on the premises?

(d) Are unofficial or voluntary funds also held in the safe?

(e) If so, does this affect the insurance position relating to official monies?

13.6 (a) Is all official money held securely, prior to its being handed to the administrative staff or cashier?

(b) Are all sums collected handed to the administrative staff or cashier the same day?

(c) Is a receipt given by the cashier or administrative staff for all collections handed to them by other staff?

13.7 Is the person in charge aware of the steps to be taken in the event of a burglary?

13.8 Is the person in charge aware of the procedure for notifying internal audit of a suspected irregularity?

13.9 Does the cash office provide sufficient protection to staff by means of:

(a) Counter grilles?

(b) Lack of access to public?

(c) Lockable tills?

(d) Alarm systems?

	Yes	No	Comments
(*e*) Any other provisions? (Specify.)			
13.10 Is the insurance cover adequate?			
13.11 Do arrangements for transporting money comply with the insurance cover?			

14. *Income due*

CALCULATION OF CHARGES

14.1 Specify which types of income arise in the department/location.

14.2 Is the basis of charge fixed by reference to:
(*a*) A statutory decision?
(*b*) A committee decision?
(*c*) A decision by a senior member of staff?
(*d*) The cost of providing the services?
(*e*) Any other means? (Specify.)

14.3 If the amount receivable is calculated in accordance with a scale of charges, has the scale been reviewed recently?
Specify:
(*a*) Minute number.
(*b*) Operative date.
(*c*) Any other authorisation.
(Attach copy of current scale.)

14.4 If the amount receivable is calculated by reference to personal means, is this in accordance with the basic scheme of assessment and has this scheme been reviewed recently?
Specify:
(*a*) Minute number.
(*b*) Operative date.

14.5 Are assessments checked by another member of staff?

14.6 Are personal circumstances regularly reviewed?

	Yes	No	Comments

14.7 (a) Who is responsible for initiating a review of the scales of charges?

(b) When were they last reviewed?

14.8 Are revisions to scales of charges implemented promptly?

14.9 If the scale is designed to recoup the full cost or a specified proportion of the cost, is the policy regarding this being adhered to?

14.10 Who is responsible for implementation of revised scales of charges once they have been approved?

CREDIT INCOME

14.11 Could the income be collected on a prepayment basis before or at the same time the service was rendered?

14.12 Is there a satisfactory system to ensure that all credit transactions are recorded and dealt with properly:

(a) For services rendered?

(b) For agreements?

(c) For specially minuted items?

(d) For other items?

14.13 Is there an adequate record to ensure that periodic or recurring charges are made?

(a) What form does this record take?

(b) Who is responsible for keeping this record?

14.14 Are debits set up to control income due?

14.15 Is this work done by:

(a) A debtor's account?

(b) An entry in an accounting record?

(c) Any other means? (Specify.)

	Yes	No	Comments
14.16 Are debtors' accounts prepared:			
(*a*) Promptly?			
(*b*) By the department concerned?			
(*c*) By the financial services department?			
(*d*) In numerical sequence?			
(*e*) To include the code to be credited?			
(*f*) To show the amount of VAT included?			
(*g*) To show the discounts allowed?			
14.17 Is the supply of debtors' accounts controlled by a department or section independent of the one raising the debit?			
14.18 How many copies of each debtor's account are prepared?			
14.19 (*a*) What is the document flow in relation to each copy?			
(*b*) If applicable, is the Treasurer's copy forwarded promptly?			
(*c*) If a copy is held at the establishment, are all payments recorded on it?			
14.20 (*a*) Are copy accounts retained for the period required for such documents?			
(*b*) In what order are they filed?			
14.21 Are debtors directed to make payments to:			
(*a*) The financial services department?			
(*b*) The department providing the service?			
(*c*) Any other location?			
14.22 Is there proper control over:			
(*a*) The cancellation of accounts?			
(*b*) The alteration of accounts?			
(*c*) The issue of credit notes?			
14.23 Is the necessary follow up action for recovery clearly laid down, and is it observed?			

	Yes	No	Comments
14.24 Where debtors pay accounts at the establishment, is the procedure for notification of overdue accounts to the Treasurer being adhered to?			
14.25 Is the financial services department responsible for the recovery of outstanding debts?			
14.26 Is the service-providing department involved at any stage in the recovery procedure? If so, specify.			
14.27 Are amendments to debits approved at a suitable senior level and in accordance with the laid-down procedure?			
14.28 Is the procedure laid down by the organisation for writing off of debts being adhered to?			
14.29 What are the provisions for writing off outstanding amounts or amending debits?			
14.30 Is there a separation of duties between the person rendering an account and those concerned with receiving the cash?			
14.31 How are sums handled which are not due to the authority?			
14.32 Is there an undue delay in the receipt of income in comparison with the earliest date it could have been received?			
14.33 (a) Is a list of bad debtors maintained to whom supplies and services will not be supplied? (b) Is it implemented?			
15. *Income estimates*			
15.1 Are income estimates prepared: (a) By heads of departments? (b) In conjunction with heads of departments?			

	Yes	No	Comments

15.2 Are these estimates in the same form as income analysis headings?

15.3 Does the chief financial officer notify heads of departments of variations from estimates.
If so:
(*a*) Is this done by way of:
(i) An exception report?
(ii) Otherwise?
(*b*) At what intervals?

15.4 Are variations from estimates promptly investigated?

15.5 Are variations required to be reported to committee?
If so, in what circumstances?

16. *Unofficial/voluntary funds*

16.1 Are the organisation's unofficial funds regulations operated?

16.2 (*a*) Are the accounts audited by the internal audit section?
(*b*) If not, are they audited by a person with relevant qualifications as required by the organisation's policy?

16.3 Is an annual financial statement and audit certificate submitted to the management committee/managers/governors in respect of each fund maintained?

If internal audit is responsible for the audit of unofficial funds, the following questions should be asked:

16.4 Are at least two persons required to sign cheques on all funds?

16.5 With trading activities (e.g. school tuckshop) are the records maintained sufficient to enable profit margins to be calculated?

	Yes	No	Comments
16.6 Where outgoings and visits are supported from unofficial funds, are detailed statements of receipts and payments prepared and signed by the teacher/person responsible?			
16.7 Are receipts issued to parents who make contributions in respect of such visits?			

APPENDIX 4
Bibliography

Publications by CIPFA's Audit Panel and available from CIPFA's Publication Department, 3 Robert Street, London WC2N 6BH

Internal audit made simple: A practical guide to successful auditing (1989)

Provides a simple and practical explanation of how to undertake a modern audit, and in the words of the author, 'to help people enjoy themselves in a really worthwhile job'. Whilst probably of most use to new or inexperienced auditors, it is nevertheless a useful refresher for all levels of staff and provides important reminders of the essentials of good auditing.

The client's view of internal audit (1990)

A research report which set out the findings of, and the issues arising from, a survey to identify managers' perceptions of their internal audit service, presently and as they saw it in the future. From this the Audit Panel identified the key issues which internal audit should address to meet the challenge of the future.

Audit report writing made simple (1991)

Poorly written reports are costly, not only in terms of the time needed to rewrite them, but also in their potential for destroying the credibility of the audit team. The main message in this guide is that a report is to persuade somebody to do something, and to do that the report must be clear and readable.

Managing computer audit (1991)

Provides useful material for those responsible for delivering a computer audit service. It is primarily aimed at the manager who is establishing a new computer audit function or who is re-evaluating an existing service.

Contract audit guidance notes (1992)

Guidance for those auditors whose organisations have entered into building contracts under the terms of the Joint Contracts Tribunal (JCT) and reflected in the JCT80 form of contract.

Measuring the performance of audit (1992)

Provides a critical assessment for both internal audit and external audit of the value of using performance measures and indicators with a range of examples.

Promoting internal audit (1992)

Describes how audit managers can review their audit departments by inviting customer feedback and then suggests how audit should present its service to potential customers.

Application of the APB 'Guidance for Internal Auditors' for local government (1993)

Provides an analysis of the duties and responsibilities of internal auditors in local authorities in England and Wales and draws upon the APB's auditing guideline *Guidance for Internal Auditors* and provides an explanation of how it can be applied within the requirements of specific local government audit legislation set down in the Accounts and Audit Regulations 1983 and Local Government Act 1972.

Computer audit guidelines (1993)

An authoritative textbook on the principles of computer audit. Now in its fourth edition and widely used throughout the public sector.

Investigating fraud in the public sector (1993)

An updated version of a guide to the procedures which should be adopted when investigating fraud.

Quality and the internal auditor (1993)

Outlines the concepts of quality, quality terminology, and quality standards together with some practical guidance on auditing in the quality environment. It describes the BS5750 process and the potential advantages of adopting quality in an arena of open competition.

Other publications

Value for money auditing (1990)

Written by Price Waterhouse and published by Gee & Co., it provides a useful overview of the subject together with examples.

Value for money audit (1990)

Published as an audit brief by the CCAB Auditing Practices Committee, this booklet provides a useful summary of VFM auditing from the external auditor's perspective. It is available from ICAEW Publications.

Index